The Karate dojo

Traditions and tales of a martial art

The Karate dojo

Traditions and tales of a martial art

by Peter Urban

Charles E. Tuttle Company

Rutland, Vermont & Tokyo, Japan

Representatives

For Continental Europe:
BOXERBOOKS, INC., Zurich
For the British Isles:
PRENTICE-HALL INTERNATIONAL, INC., London
For Australasia:
BOOK WISE (AUSTRALIA) PTY. LTD.
104–108 Sussex Street, Sydney 2000

Published by the Charles E. Tuttle Company, Inc.,
of Rutland, Vermont, and Tokyo, Japan
with editorial offices at
Suido 1-chome, 2-6, Bunkyo-ku, Tokyo

This book is respectfully dedicated to my dear friend, Professor Richard Kim of San Francisco, without whose help and guidance it would never have evolved.

The author wishes to express his deepest appreciation to Roy Colonna of New York City for his Karate drawings, and to James Brown and Joan R. Brochstein of Tokyo for their patience and immeasurable assistance in bringing the original manuscript to life.

Contents

The weaponless weapon

Karate is a martial art, a concept, a way of life new to the western world. Despite its grand and long-lived tradition in the Orient, Karate has until recently been unknown to most of the world's population; only in the past decade have Americans become aware of this fascinating art of self-defense. In the pages of this book, we shall discover why Karate is now flourishing throughout the world, why it has become a modus vivendi for millions of martial arts devotees.

Karate owes its profound impact on Americans to the promoters of the mass media, who realized the potential excitement such a sport could engender and who therefore gave it maximum exposure. By means of television, motion pictures, newspapers, and magazines, a new hero image has been implanted in the American mind. No longer is man's strength limited to the weapon he carries: he now possesses the "weaponless weapon," his own body, and all feats of prowess are possible. Americans are becoming conscious of the fact that their physical capabilities are dependent upon individual determination. The widespread publicity of Karate is responsible for the increasing numbers of people who have become confident in their ability to fight, to hold their own in a society of competition.

Perhaps the most significant result of the growing awareness of Karate is the realization among educators that here is an unexplored area of knowledge: there is much to be learned about Karate as a practical means of self-defense, as a sport, and as a philosophy. The American parent too has become aware of the necessity of equipping his children with a knowledge of the martial arts if they are to develop fully—mentally as well as physically. The art of self-defense has been virtually ignored by families and by schools; these social institutions now believe that it must be included in a realistic approach to education. Karate teachers in particular have been appalled by society's lack of concern for the welfare of its youth.

One of the great problems facing American society today is lack of respect for authority; it has become common for teenagers to harrass policemen and teachers. It is apparent that such power figures are ill-equipped to defend themselves to their maximum capacity against those who would challenge them. Since a child's respect for an adult often has strength as its basis, it is essential that all adults who deal with children be physically competent. The youngster who is reared in an atmosphere of shootings and knifings would perhaps emerge from childhood as a better citizen if as a youth he felt respect for those in authority. In later years, the fact that his respect was originally based on the physical prowess of his elders would not be important; the fact would remain that he did respect them. The blackboard jungle that is all too common in American cities would

A good Karateman develops first of all his katas to perfection; then broadens his character accordingly.

cease to exist if teenagers knew that their teachers' knowledge encompassed more than history or mathematics, that they also had knowledge of the art of self-defense.

If Karate were to be made a natural part of one's education, much of the unhappiness and neurosis so prevalent today would disappear; crime would inevitably be reduced. The unspoken taboo against physically trained women would be lifted, and the defenseless women of today would be capable of defending themselves in any situation.

Americans who had served in the Far East during World War II and the Korean War introduced Karate to the United States. Despite the widespread opinion that Karate was merely a fad which would soon pass from the national scene, this unique sport captured lasting interest in America. Since World War II, thousands of Americans have adopted Karate wholeheartedly as a way of life, as a means of self-defense, or simply as a rewarding physical development program. The latter is especially true of businessmen and theatrical people, who depend so heavily upon health, appearance, and psychic confidence for competitive success.

Karate is filling two vital needs previously unrecognized in American society: the human needs to express emotion, and to live without fear. Americans, taught from childhood to suppress their feelings, often acquire psychological problems; through a martial art such as Karate, young people find an outlet for aggression and learn not to fear emotions.

Young men of draft age are now training in Karate by the thousands in order to be as well prepared as possible for the service. Such training can never be a mistake; the advantage of having the weaponless weapon speaks for itself in this instance. Countless college students are studying Karate, keenly aware of its usefulness throughout life. Having realized the value of the martial arts, increasing numbers of police academies are experimenting with its techniques; Karate training is now provided for many policemen in the large cities.

Physicians too have become well aware of the worth of Karate and are prescribing such a program as therapy for many of their patients. Over the years, it has been noted that those who practice Karate are rarely ill and are generally more vigorous than the average person. Not only does Karate training improve one's health physically, it also benefits one's mental attitude. New-found confidence is a prize which a Karateman acquires soon after the inception of his training. Physical strength attained in a short period of time has decided effects upon the individual. A most interesting observation is that in many cases individuals appear to have rapidly attained maturity through their study of Karate. Many parents have observed that Karate causes their young sons to become men very quickly: in some cases parental control can no longer be maintained by resorting to physical superiority.

Karate training is based on rigid discipline, a factor which limits the number of students who will ever achieve high proficiency. The rigorous training soon alienates certain types of people; those who dislike hard work, discipline, or competition soon lose interest. To excel in Karate is an achievement most valued by people who are highly realistic.

Karate tournaments are an ever-growing source of entertainment to sports fans of all types. When Karate becomes as popular as bowling or golf, the United States will have become a Karate-oriented nation. It will never replace boxing, wrestling, or other combative sports, but will instead enhance their appeal.

Karate societies and organizations, as well as societies dedicated to other martial arts, are springing up all over America, filling the social needs of individual and community alike. Despite its competitiveness, Karate training develops a feeling of brotherhood among its adherents; great rapport soon exists between brothers. Dojos are the freemason organizations of the martial arts; the training hall is a lodge, a home for the devotee. It opens many other worlds to students: the world of physical well-being, the world of social contacts, the world of self-confidence where fear has no place.

The most defamatory arguments leveled against Karate are made by critics who have unfortunately been exposed to inferior demonstrations or who were themselves unsuccessful in Karate training. It has been called savage, barbaric, uncivilized, phony. Karate devotees comfort themselves in the fact that all new knowledge goes through a period of doubt and ridicule before sufficient exposure causes the true picture to emerge.

Karate was once considered an esoteric Oriental subject of unknown origin whose main requirement was that its practitioners beat parts of their bodies on inanimate objects for the purpose of developing hardened limbs and the ability to destroy material things. This erroneous image is

"The Karate philosophy of calmness and confidence is the antithesis of aggression and inhumanity."

why Karate has been so maligned; in fact, the image of the animalistic, barbaric Karateman is an absurdity, for the Karate philosophy of calmness and confidence is the antithesis of aggression and inhumanity to man. Through the efforts of thousands of dedicated practitioners, the essence of Karate has at long last been brought to light; in spite of misrepresentation, Karate has achieved national acceptance in a relatively short time.

There are many kinds of martial arts and many kinds of Karate. At present there are over forty popular styles of Karate training. Nevertheless, in depth they are all basically the same, for the goal does not vary according to style; it is always the same, to become a more balanced person. In the long run, Karate becomes like the people who use it; each individual gravitates to the style most befitting his taste. Differences between styles occur because of their adherents' concepts and approaches toward training methods. Occasionally, a Karateman will become involved with more than one style.

Karatemen are notoriously proud, and justifiably so, considering the lengths to which a devotee must go. The competition which naturally arises between Karatemen sometimes prevents mutual understanding, for each man's goal is to excel. Although there is occasional friction between adherents, the sense of competitiveness insures the continued growth and improvement of Karate.

Instruction in the martial arts is one of the newest professions to evolve in the social structure. To be a professional Karate teacher of the first calibre requires at least fifteen years of study and practice. It is extraordinarily demanding work which would be considered impractical by those who would expect lucrative returns from such enormous input; but to those who are truly devoted to the Karate way of life, the rewards of the work itself are enough.

This book was written with the hope that those wishing to understand and follow "the way" of Karate will seek out a dojo suitable for them. If such a dojo does not exist, it will be found one way or another, for in Karatedo (way of Karate) "nothing is impossible."

The dojo

Karate is taught in a school called a dojo. More than merely a gymnasium or a club, a dojo is a cherished place of learning and brotherhood for Karate devotees. But the word "dojo" implies an even broader meaning: to the dedicated student, the dojo soon becomes a concept, a way of life. The word is symbolic of the methodological, the ideological, the philosophical aspects of Karate. Thus, the study of Karate involves far more than the learning of certain physical techniques; it absorbs the student wholly; his character is as much affected by Karate as is his body.

Karate is one aspect of the martial arts, a collective system of combatives which derive their common ancestry from the Orient. "Combative" is a term describing a physical or physiodynamic system of the training of the mind and the body according to certain principles. The principles vary with each system: some systems employ wood and metal instruments as weapons, considering them to be merely an extension of the body. By learning the use of weapons, Karatemen prepare themselves to fight barehanded against them. Karate, Kenpo, Kung-fu, Tai-chi-chuan, Judo, Jiu-Jitsu, Bo-Jitsu, Aikido, and Kendo are examples of such systems. There are also sub-systems of each one. Within Karate, there are various methodologies, or methods, known as "ryus."

Karate, translated as "empty hand," deals primarily in developing the body so as to bring about a practiced control of the limbs and in developing certain mental energies (sometimes called "ki," "kime," "kiai," "chi") so as to make the body into a highly effective tool of the mind: the body becomes in effect a weaponless weapon. The mental demands in rigorous Karate training are more taxing than the physical demands.

It is necessary at this point to delineate the differences between Eastern and Western martial arts. "Martial" is defined in English as: "pertaining to war, military training for the purpose of war." In the Orient, on the other hand, martial art originated as a means of attaining physical good health and longevity as well as a philosophical or spiritual goal. Combative training is not the sole purpose, as is often the case in the West; it is a beginning rather than an end.

In the past, Western cultures have experienced manifestations of martial arts, or fighting arts, as seen in the English Round Table legends and in the Norse and Greek myths. Although men have fought for a principle or a religion, the martial art of the Western cultures has rarely developed to the point of embodying an individual philosophy. Due to this lack of philosophical content in military training, the term "martial art" is a misnomer in the West; the term "military science" is more applicable. Karate is considered an art by its practitioners rather than a fighting science. Besides their philosophical basis, martial arts sometimes have religious foundations, usually a form of Buddhist theology. This is primarily the case in remote areas of China, where Karate began, and in Japan. In the instances where this occurs, the ideas of the particular sect are included in the methodology and rationale of the art itself.

The most commonly accepted role of the individual likewise differs in the Eastern and Western concepts of martial art. In military science, conformity of action is essential. All decisions are made according to echelons of authority. Individual initiative is seldom required. But in the martial arts, an individual is a single fighting unit complete unto himself. His actions are governed by his intuitive judgment: there is neither punishment nor reward for his effort or lack of it. One's initiative determines the degree of skill, knowledge, spirit, and how the three are integrated. There is, however, a certain affinity between Eastern and Western martial arts when compared on a realistic rather than on a conceptual basis; the reactions of individuals vary and cannot be considered in broad generalizations.

Although the term "martial arts" means fighting arts, a truer interpretation of its Oriental meaning may be found in the Japanese word "Budo," which, freely translated, implies "the way of the fighter." The suffix "do" or "way," which is so often used in Chinese and Japanese religious thought (in Chinese it is sometimes called "Tao"), does not mean only the learning and application of techniques and skills. Its meaning is more profound; the spiritual use of the techniques and the integration of these techniques with the spirit are all-important. A "way" or "path" is intended to lead the individual to the attainment of perfection or what is often known as self-realization, enlightenment, or simply maturity.

The spirit of the martial arts today is the last vestige of the spirit of the Zen warriors of old. They were the purveyors of a great morality and code of manhood. Contrary to many critics' opinions, trained killers or expendable soldiers are not the end results of martial arts training. Rather, martial arts students eventually take on the spirit of the old warriors and become great, highly spirited men.

There are beautiful stories from ancient times about samurai (the sword-wielding knights of old Japan) who saved themselves from death at the hands of another samurai by composing and reciting an impromptu poem. If, with the point of a sword at his throat, the bushi (knight) recited a poem that met with the rigid rules and was entirely original and spontaneous, his life would be spared by the other. This was a test of courage and equanimity in the face of almost certain death.

Because of this spiritual attitude, which was encountered, nurtured, and grown to flower in the dojo, a real samurai never surrendered or asked for mercy: he was incapable of squirming in the face of death. He was able to respond to conditions around him with objectivity and calm detachment, even while being intimately involved in them.

The highest achievement for a samurai was the attainment of virtue. The hallmarks of this virtue were relaxation, even-mindedness, pride, confidence, and graciousness. All traditional dojos today which teach any form of martial art, be it Karate, Kendo, Judo, Ju-Jitsu, archery, or others, are based on this idea of virtue; indeed, the followers of the martial arts today are in effect the descendents of the samurai of old. It is the aim of all martial arts masters to work toward the promulgation of this spirit of the ancient Zen warriors, a spirit which is much more than mere knowledge of fighting techniques: it is the attainment of a virtuous way of life. Karate can be considered as a philosophy based on the belief that a sound mind is achieved through the development of a virtuous character. A sound body is achieved through rigorous training. The natural result of sound mind and sound body is "oneness": the oneness of Zen (mind) and Ken (fist or body); Zen, Ken, Ishoa: mind, fist, oneness.

True Karatemen believe that learning and excellence cannot stand still. They believe that one must do what one cannot do. They believe in the old standards of excellence wherein to excel is the common goal of all. They increase their efforts and raise their goals as each step toward excellence is achieved. Their Karate training is reflected in every aspect of their daily living. As Karatemen train their bodies to make them stronger and healthier, they develop their characters accordingly; they then transcend the limits of the physical. The origin of Karate was the development of a way to free the ego from the limitations of physical equality.

A traditional dojo is, in a sense, a patriarchy. The "sensei" is the master of the dojo. "Sensei" is the Japanese word for "honorable teacher" but is also used in Japan

"A way to free the ego from the limitations of physical equality."

to denote doctors and lawyers, for doctors are considered to be teachers (of the way of health) and lawyers are considered to be teachers (of the way of law). The sensei regards his students as his many sons and daughters, seeing them as they can never see themselves. He effects the development of their bodies and characters—this is the responsibility of his art. The dojo is really the home of the sensei; students come to his home to learn his way of life. That way of life is Karate.

A sensei must always be an example of high virtue. His relationships with his many students must be, above all, objective and well defined. Only in this way is the perpetual learning and improvement process kept intact. Since all martial arts training is primarily oriented toward the spirit of self-reliance, it is the sensei's obligation to set an example for his students in all things: in excellence, discipline, moderation, and wisdom. A sensei thoroughly learns the art of helping himself before he obtains the ability to help others. Often in the course of training, a student reaches a standstill in his development due to excessive ambition, impatience, fear of failure, or for other emotional and psychological reasons. According to the situation, the sensei is then required to become a counselor or a friend, as well as a teacher, in order to aid in solving the individual's problems in development. Over-training is just as profitless as under-training: too much effort is an indication that a student has lost faith in himself; lack of effort is identified with giving up. The sensei gives recognition and confidence when deserved, strong honest criticism when necessary. All senseis are perfectionists; thus, com-

"Competition keeps the Karate student geared to the art all his life."

pliments are rare in a real Karate school. Every student learns to take it for granted that the basic requirement for continual development is to put forth his utmost effort at all times.

Maintaining their bodies in top physical condition is mandatory for all students. They are required to fight long bouts with skilled and unskilled fighters every night. They are made to practice auto-suggestion and meditation. They learn that winners never quit and quitters never win. It usually takes several years of proving themselves in the dojo before the students are befriended by the sensei. Excuses are never accepted, and the demands on students are always increased as the students improve. Professor

Rules in a Karate dojo:
1. Everyone works.
2. Nothing is free.
3. All start at the bottom.

Richard Kim, a great sensei, once said about Karate training, "It is the challenge that makes lifetime devotees of the art." The challenge is from oneself and to oneself.

All traditional dojos are created by the sensei and maintain the standards of simplicity and beauty found in the original dojos. In the dojos of old Japan, the quality of work performed was a reflection of the atmosphere within the dojo. A typically Japanese Karate dojo is spacious, immaculate, and structurally beautiful. Some of the older training halls have art objects displayed, in keeping with martial arts traditions. When it is impossible for a sensei to obtain such pieces, he will use whatever materials are available, such as stone, metal, cloth, or wood, to create an atmosphere of dignity and excellence for his students. The original dojos always had a shrine built in the highest possible position, symbolizing the dojo's dedication to the virtues and values of its Karate style.

All martial arts dojos have time allotted for the practice of meditation. In some, it precedes and ends the training sessions; in others it is practiced only at the end of training. A good student will spend several years in the dojo before he develops the ability to clear his mind completely of all thoughts at will. It is difficult in the beginning to think of nothing. Some students start by concentrating on a mental picture that is easy to imagine; often they choose the image of a light bulb. With his eyes closed, the student concentrates on remembering how a lighted bulb looks. The body is relaxed in the formal seated position. By concentrating only on the mental image, one finds it easy to exclude all other thoughts. This is a beginning technique; eventually the practice of meditation techniques leads one to the ability to clear the mind and relax the body instantly. Many college students tell their senseis of the beneficial effect of their practice of meditation when they have examinations; they find themselves able to clear their minds of all worries and nervousness before they start their tests. They invariably achieve successes that they never thought possible.

It is not surprising that Karate students are rarely ill, for they know that it is necessary to use the body and the mind every day in order to function at their best. The atmosphere in the dojo is one of energy: it is considered a great loss of face for a student to lag behind the pace of his fellow students. They learn not to show pain when injured in sparring and never to show weariness. Such systematic physical disciplines, in conjunction with the group competitive system for status, work for the furtherance of physical health and strength of character.

During training the students wear a cloth headband known as the "hachimaki." Its practical use is to keep one's hair from becoming disheveled and to prevent perspiration from running into the eyes; it is especially useful during intensive summer training. The hachimaki also has a more profound meaning: it is the symbol of one's dedication to the hard work necessary to train correctly. The meaning of the hachimaki is akin to the Western gesture of rolling up the sleeves. It symbolizes the seriousness of getting down to business. The hachimaki is a constant reminder that one must never train half-heartedly.

Imagine that you are entering a dojo for the first time.

"It is considered a great loss of face to lag behind the pace."

"The young masters are respected, but the old masters are venerated."

The following is typical of what you could expect to see:

When the clock strikes the hour, the senior man signals the beginning of formal training. The students quickly form ranks, standing close together in a militaristic posture. Suddenly, not a sound can be heard. Everyone drops smartly to the floor in the formal sitting position and awaits the coming of the sensei.

Their attitude is alert when he approaches his place. Japanese professors of Karate usually give their students a test of discipline at this point by slowly and dramatically assuming the sitting position. In some elaborate dojos, especially in a Kendo dojo, the sensei will use the time to put on his gear and tie his belt. It is a ceremonial procedure used primarily to test the patience and composure of the students. The higher the rank of the teacher, the more elaborate are the formalities. Depending on the teacher's rank in the system, his students call him "sensei" or "sheehan," which denote "teacher" and "professor" respectively. The young masters are respected, but the old masters are venerated.

When the master is ready, the senior student calls out in a strong voice words that mean "All bowing to the teacher." Everyone's forehead touches the floor. As they do this, they energetically recite words which mean, "Please instruct us, sensei." The professor then returns the bow, bowing deeper and more humbly than all the rest.

The group training commences with scientifically designed loosening-out and warming-up exercises, followed by chest, arms, and stomach-building work, with the emphasis on endurance. Progression is then made to a physical statement, or demonstration, of all basic forms, such as the punching and blocking techniques. They are done in a slow, rhythmical fashion to the almost hypnotically chanting voice of the leader. Students appear to be gliding through the motions. Their fists are rock-hard while exercising this controlled dynamic tension motion study in unison. The chant enables the entire group, skilled professional athletes as well as beginners, to train together. The demands of the chanter force the correct movement and proper speed.

In formal Karate training, the sound of the training chant can be easily distinguished. It consists of a particular strength of intonation and hypnotic emphasis on certain rhythms which are conducive to the most articulate performance of the hand and foot techniques. Ballet teachers have this ability, but, unlike the ballet master, the good Karate chanter can lead the instruction and physical training for very long periods of time. He can vary the pace of the workout to include the strenuous work called "maximum effort repetitions" and the relaxing work called "slow gliding articulations." In this fashion, a group in hard physical training exercise can rest while they are still working.

The beginning soft chant is suddenly followed by a stronger hard chant. This is the signal to begin a number of repetitions in which everyone expounds his maximum effort and speed. In this manner Karate students go from one technique to the other, night after night, year after year. Only the most imaginative Karate students ever learn to correctly call the chant. The Japanese drill masters are the most outstanding chanters in the world, for they have a certain twang in their voice which is not heard anywhere else. If a dojo produces one or two excellent chanters in five years, it is exceptional, for such men are rare.

The training leader makes transitions from one speed to another and from one exercise to another, continually varying between hard and soft. He can cover the best techniques in a short time with great benefit to all. This continues in a strong dojo for at least an hour and a half every night. Some martial arts men train six nights a week at that pace.

One's mind has no time to be troubled in a tough Karate workout. The use of one's strengths and energies, the revitalizing effect of the Karate breathing, and the satisfaction of having to fight many other people, followed by relaxation and meditation practices, make Karate students feel a robust sense of good health at all times.

All beginners in Karate training learn from intimate experience how sprains and bruises feel, what causes them, and how they are to be avoided in learning the art of fighting. This elementary training lasts until they become completely at home with fighting motions and emotions.

Training phases run in periods of approximately three months; in each period a particular development, such as the blocking system, is emphasized. In the course of a year, all four aspects of training—the blocking system, the training dances, the fighting, and the physical conditioning—are individually emphasized. Training in most dojos takes place in the evening. Punctuality is a must; students who are in the habit of being late are not permitted to train.

"Karate is considered an art by its practitioners rather than a fighting science."

After reaching the higher levels of achievement, the three basic types of Karate men are perfected: punchers, kickers, and dancers. To be fully oriented in Karate, however, a student must develop an enormous facility in all three. This can be achieved only by diligent work on the makiwara (striking device), frequent participation in the jiu-kumite (sparring) matches, and intensive practice of the katas (dances).

Each style of Karate has its code of character-building to which all students aspire. An example of the virtues a student may hope to acquire in his dojo are the five virtues of the Goju way. At the conclusion of formal training, all students are seated in the meditation position in front of the sensei. They recite in unison the guiding principles of their style. The following is the meaning of what they say:

"We who are studying Karate do aspire to these virtues:

1. We are proud to study the spirit of Goju.
2. We shall always practice courtesy.
3. We shall be quick to seize opportunity.
4. We shall always practice patience.
5. We shall always keep the fighting spirit of Karate."

The students then listen attentively to the words of criticism and praise coming from the sparkling face of the old grand master, who has lived the dojo life, just like this, every day for over half a century.

He dismisses the evening's training after the meditation ceremonies are accomplished, usually closing with words that sound like "Go-kuro-san" ("Thank you for doing what is expected of you"). These words are a contraction which indicates the teacher's seniority when he returns courtesies to juniors. The proper term, "Go-kuro-sama deshita" ("Thank you for your troubles") is not common in daily dojo formalities.

A true Karateka (Karate person) reaches the zenith of training when he can conquer the unyielding with the yielding. One invariably asks, "How can a yielding object conquer an unyielding object?" This can best be illustrated by a famous Karate lesson, to wit: "There is nothing in life more yielding than a whiff of air or a drop of water, but who can withstand the force of a typhoon or a tidal wave?" The typhoon and the tidal wave are nothing more than the mass movements of air and water, which had their beginnings in a single whiff of air or a single drop of water, pliable and yielding. A Karateka is relaxed, physically at ease, spiritually enlightened, but has the capability of raising himself to the heights of a raging typhoon or a towering tidal wave, sweeping away every obstacle when his life or the lives of those he loves are in danger.

Karatemen all develop the art of complete relaxation, for they learn to use their training and spiritual concepts in every aspect of their daily lives. Profound personality changes occur as new students develop fighting ability. The introvert finds that he has become brave, the overly aggressive personality becomes calm. Karate training has the power to destroy neurosis and integrate and broaden the character. Confidence becomes evident in students' everyday living; they take pride in their physical strength.

Posture, agility, breathing, and coordination become of vital concern. The vigorous exercises expand their chests and broaden their shoulders, and fat is replaced by muscle. Their threshold of sensitivity to minor pain diminishes to zero, along with emotionally-induced illnesses and those resulting from insufficient physical activity. Their endurance level rises, causing them to accomplish great amounts of work. Taught a doctrine of living wherein health and happiness go hand in hand, students enjoy hard work and exercise. They learn that the best way to be happy is to make others happy; perhaps this is why all mature Kara-temen are excellent fathers and permanent family men.

To graduate from a traditional Japanese dojo is the most rewarding experience in a student's life. Receiving his diploma for a given grade of achievement is a thrill which a student eagerly anticipates. After a formal examination and evaluation, the degree master of the dojo posts great white scrolls on the dojo wall giving the names of those who have received a high enough evaluation for advancement to the next grade. In preparing for the ceremony, one readies his best uniform so that it is in perfect condition in order to make the grandest possible appearance in front of his sensei, his fellow students, and the throng of visitors.

The formal ceremonies in these dojos are a great and solemn affair. Since they often last in excess of forty minutes, students practice keeping the formal sitting posture for sustained periods of time long in advance of the occasion itself. To change to a comfortable position or to show discomfort in any way during the ceremony is a complete loss of face. One's back must be as straight as a ramrod, his shoulders squared, his chest thrown out, his chin high, his eyes looking straight ahead at all times.

Sometimes a retired grand patriarch is a guest at such an event. He of course says a few words of inspiration to the successful students receiving a degree. Such a speaker is usually past eighty years of age and finds it appropriate at such an occasion to call upon his storehouse of memories and to weave stories of the past for his audience. This is a terrifying occurrence for the Karate students, for they know that the old patriarch can sit in the formal position for many hours without the slightest discomfort: the young students all hope that lightning will strike or an earthquake will occur so that they can change their position before the circulation in their legs stops forever.

Upon receiving their degrees, honor students are given a thunderous ovation by the audience. Following the ceremony, there is usually a four-hour recess followed by an elaborate party in the dojo to initiate those who have attained their first black belt degree. The new black belters, or shodans, are required to fight jiu-kumite all night long with other new shodans from the various prefectures who have made the annual trip to the main dojo. The masters and the high-ranking dans (black belters) sip warm rice wine (sake) all night and sing and dance. The shodans spend the next two days sleeping and taking hot baths. A similar type of party is held in the Japanese dojo each New Year's Day, when the families of the Karatemen are invited; this is the most beloved of all holidays.

A Karate dojo becomes famous on the basis of its standards. The differences between the major Karate styles and between the various martial arts lie not in the divergence of their concepts, but rather in the varying opinions and standards of excellence. In Chinese Kenpo, the forerunner of Karate, training standards were so high and the resulting fighting techniques so brilliant that secrecy could be maintained only by permitting none but members to enter their dojos.

The Chinese teachers were known by a name pronounced "seefu," which corresponds to the Japanese "sensei." Applicants often waited several years before a master decided that the potential students had enough patience. The demands placed upon students to achieve excellence were unusually stringent; a man calling himself a "serious student" would have had from twenty to forty years of experience.

On the occasions of martial arts exhibitions in the old Orient, there was often a "Shinken Shobu," a fight to the death held between rival champions of different societies. They were real duels that often resulted in the death of one or both opponents. Although the British authorities put a stop to this practice in Hong Kong many years ago, it is still a frequent occurrence in isolated parts of the mainland. The jiu-kumite of Karate as we know it today was not practiced in the Chinese arts; their contests were never sporting events, but were always real duels. Some of the fiercest fights known to mankind have taken place at these Chinese martial arts exhibitions.

Those students who failed to put forth their best effort at all times were often expelled from the Karate societies for a period of not less than two years. If a student was disrespectful toward a Japanese master or a senior dan, the most formidable black belters in the dojo would take him bodily and shave off his hair and eyebrows. They would then throw him naked into the street where all the students in the dojo would pelt him with stones. If, after two years, such a disrespectful student had come to a change of attitude, it was possible for him to be readmitted into the Karate society.

In the ancient days of Japan and China, certain holy men from time to time appeared in the towns on holidays. Dressed in beautiful costumes of brilliantly colored silks, the leaders of the group usually gave a short speech explaining that they were holy men from the nearby monastery and that once a year they put on an exhibition of their unique talents. They hoped the viewers would be pleased and generously donate whatever money they could for the needs of the monastery.

Few spectacles in the world were as beautiful or as exciting as these events. Men were seen ripping the bark off trees with merely their fingertips. There were ferocious fights between handlers of nine foot poles. Other men would fight several opponents simultaneously. Some smashed huge rocks to bits with their bare fists. Occasionally a few small animals would be killed by the power of the Karatemen's scream, for it was strong enough to shock or frighten a small creature to death. Besides amusing and amazing the spectators, it also frightened many to the point that they spontaneously urinated in their clothing.

The training dances (katas) were strangely beautiful. As

many as fifty men, costumed, wearing masks, and brandishing all kinds of fighting weapons, would perform the dances to the intricate, hypnotic rhythms of twenty or more huge drums, gongs, and cymbals, together with the strange, haunting sounds of the Chinese woodwind instruments.

At the present time in the Chinese section of any large metropolis in the world one still sees semblances of these dances, performed on festival days in memory of the old arts and those who practiced them. The participants are a clan of the most successful professional and business men, who have practiced the arts called "Kung-fu" or "Tai-chi-chuan" since their youth. Members of these clans, called Dragon or Benevolent Societies, often lead physically active and healthy lives well into their nineties. Each society owns two or more effigies of dragons constructed out of paper, cloth, papier-mâché, and carved wood, the more elaborate dragons being as much as one hundred feet in length. Using the techniques and training of the old martial arts, the strongest and most skillful members place themselves inside the effigy, guiding and directing the dragon's movements. Under the control of a skillful group of dancers, the movements of the "dance of the dragon" become uncannily realistic and lifelike, the dragon performing incredible feats of agility, such as stretching its body up the side of a building to the third or fourth floor in order to accept the offering of a "string of money" placed there by a merchant for good luck in the coming year. This feat is accomplished by means of a human pyramid, requiring excellent timing and balance.

Training in the old days of Japan was far more severe

than the training of today. The traditional Japanese spirit, known as "Yamato Damashii" (Japan Spirit), is equivalent to our own "never say die" Yankee spirit. In those early days, there were interesting training aids which were used to build a solid foundation in strength and discipline. One of these was a bamboo pole used during kicking practice which was supported on the shoulders of each student in the fashion of a yoke. Ropes attached to both ends of the yoke held buckets full of water. The total weight of the device was about thirty pounds; the average weight of the students was one-hundred and twenty pounds. They had to shoulder the yokes and stand in neat ranks under the stern direction of the drill master, who carried a split bamboo stick about three feet in length known as the "cudgel of inspiration." Any student who went amiss and spilled water on the dojo floor as a result of poor balance and effort would be politely admonished, then given a solid whack of the bamboo pole across the backside. It was such rigid discipline which gave them their superb balance and kicking ability.

Sometimes students would faint, especially those who did not keep themselves in perfect physical condition. In fact, some of the teachers who knew only the hard school would use fainting as a criterion to gauge the amount of effort being put forth by their students.

Training during the summer months was nearly unbearable in those days, for the temperature was frequently above one hundred degrees, and there was no relaxation in work standards. But the situation in the summer was considered a luxury compared with training during the

34

"He unwittingly changes his way of life, for he can never be the same person again."

winter. Freezing weather, no heaters of any type, and outdoor benjos (toilets) were standard. Students had to do their makiwara training (punching the striking post) outside in the snow, rain, sleet, and hail with bare feet and wearing only their thin Karate uniform. This aspect of training was known as "building internal fortitude." The older students who had developed their internal fortitude were seemingly impervious to such discomfort. It was considered impolite to complain about the cold of winter or the heat of summer; likewise, good manners in the dojo dictated that, in the case of injury, all were supposed to pretend that nothing had happened. Students who had sustained painful injuries displayed neither pain nor panic. Their only concern was to avoid losing face by having someone help them or by interfering with those still fighting.

To be a teacher in those days, one had to be able to set bones, pull dislocations, stop bleeding, and deal with many types of emotional and physical injuries. It was so rough that students never made plans for the hours after training.

Dojos were usually located in the poorer sections of town, and naturally the local village roughnecks would try to single out individual Karate students for some sport. The real jiu-kumite (fighting practice) would occur on the way home from that part of town.

Thus, the building called "dojo," housing the complex world of Karate, is a shell wherein the individual first experiences the life of competition and challenge. He unwittingly changes his way of life, for he can never be the same person again.

The belt system

The martial arts method of evaluating merit and development is known as the belt system, with the color of the belts designating the various steps of attainment. In Karate the system is divided into two basic categories: the lower level is called "kyu," implying the idea of "boy"; the upper level is called "dan," implying the idea of "man." As a student of Karate develops physically, he is expected to broaden his character accordingly. The requirements for each level vary in each Karate style and in each dojo according to the sensei's standards, which reflect the degree of perfection which he demands of himself.

The white belt denotes the beginner. There are usually three steps which the student must attain before he can attain the next belt level. A superior student is able successfully to complete the requirements after three or four months of intensive training. The qualifications include excellence in the following: primary physical conditioning, standard training procedure of the style, basic fighting forms, and the rudimentary training dances, or katas. The students are motivated to do well by a status system: they see that the color of the belt changes as their abilities and accomplishments increase.

The senior white belters are easily identified. They take pride in their uniforms and keep them well laundered. After the first few months, it becomes a mark of honor to have a frayed belt, for the seniors are anxious to differentiate themselves from the newer students.

In most styles, students begin the climb, as white belts, on a scale that begins with the eighth kyu and advances in descending progression. The first important accomplishment of a student is advancement to the green belt level. This level encompasses two stages of primary development: the lower, called the fifth kyu; the upper, called the fourth kyu. It is with an intense feeling of pride in his achievement that a student receives his new rank of green belt. He realizes that he has accomplished the first of a long series of steps leading to the heights he wishes to attain. Training for these students becomes more intense. Their focusing power (punching power) starts to develop. Green belters continuously practice sparring with the other colored belters in their school; they have learned how to fight without causing unnecessary injuries. When accidents do occur, as invariably they will, they are shrugged off as meaningless. Many white belters (about sixty per cent) quit before they make their green colors, for Karate training is so difficult in the beginning that most people find it easier to quit than to continue. The purple belt follows the green belt, but not all styles use it, however.

The brown belt represents the ripening maturity of the developing student. In most dojos, the brown belt has three levels, starting at the third kyu and progressing up to the first kyu, which denotes a first class student. Brown belters show the most aggression in sparring and always seem to be the hardest workers, for they have begun to realize that just being good and practicing daily is not enough. Their main concern is to become worthy of advancement to first degree black belt. Their many hours of strenuous work and discipline have taught them that nothing in Karate or in life comes easily, that learning, excellence, and achievement must always be pursued. Brown belters take pride in drilling new students, and they compete in every dojo contest and Karate tournament, thus getting the experience necessary to fulfill the requirements for black belt.

Few students progress beyond the brown belt level. This stage in development, which is referred to as the "jumping off place," separates the men from the boys. Satisfied with their accomplishments, many students become permanent or temporary drop-outs.

The first degree black belter is called the "shodan," meaning "first man" in Japanese. Achievement identification now changes from low numbers to high numbers, the inverse of the kyu system. First degree is the bottom of a ladder which progresses up to ten, although in some Karate styles the terminal grade is between five and ten.

Of the small number of Karate students who pursue the shodan degree, even fewer completely develop the grade. Under optimum conditions, in an excellent, strictly disciplined dojo, the shodan degree can be earned in a period of two to three years.

First dans are the core of a strong fighting dojo. Since they set the example for the lower grades, there are many pressures and demands made on them by their teacher, and they must participate in as much sparring competition as possible. It is a source of great satisfaction and pride for a sensei to watch a student develop over the years from a kyu to a dan. He realizes a sense of fulfillment in the work of producing a good Karateka, and a unique teacher-student relationship develops which lasts all their lives.

The second dan rank, the degree above shodan, is called "nidan" in Japanese, meaning "second man." Some styles use intermediary, or half, steps, which are called "ho" grades in Japanese. "Nidan-ho" designates that the students are in the process of developing the abilities to meet the requirements for the full grade. In a good dojo of a strict Karate system, a superior student may make the second dan rank in a period of four years of total training. Very few of a dojo's students make it to this level. At this point, they are highly experienced fighters, having fought thousands of sparring matches in their school and at tournaments. But now their main concern is to perfect their katas. Karate has become for them a way of life, and they are extremely proud men.

Second dans in the dojo are the right arm of the sensei; they conduct the training and do the fundamental teaching, bringing beginning students to the point where they are ready to enter the main class under the direction of the sensei. Many years of experience in teaching under the guidance of the sensei are required before they can obtain a franchise to practice teaching outside of their parent dojo.

The nidans learn the superior techniques of style from the sensei privately. As their jiu-kumite (sparring) has become quite strong, they delight in rough fighting bouts, especially with the first dans. In major Karate tournaments, this division usually does the most exciting fighting and wins the most trophies.

In a good dojo it takes at least six years of total training to attain the third dan, or third degree black belt, level, called "sandan." Karatemen on this level are highly respected and are referred to in their dojos as "dai-sempai," or "number one older brothers." In traditional systems, the students in a dojo feel like younger and older brothers to one another, a custom which is not concerned with chronological age, but refers rather to one's skills and ability.

The requirements for the sandan level vary in different schools, but generally require that a student have completed at least six years of training and mastered at least fourteen katas of native and foreign styles in addition to having won a first or second place championship in a tournament of national or international importance.

The use of various karate fighting instruments is taught to the sandans. They keep very secret all the special knowledge imparted to them by their sensei, jealously guarding what they have worked so hard and so long to learn. On formal nights in the dojo, they occasionally spar with the junior black belters, it being their custom to soundly thrash all opponents with a stern, big-brother attitude. This is a great morale booster for the other students; it is an honor as well as a slight trauma for the junior grades to fight with the highly experienced sandans. When one has attained this level, he has earned the equivalent of a bachelor of science degree and is considered a true instructor.

In the Gojuryu Karate system, the fourth and fifth dan levels can be recognized by the half-red, half-white belt; the fourth dans wear the belt with the red facing down, the fifth dans with the red facing up. Both classes are called "renshi" in Japanese, meaning "senior expert"; fourth dan is considered low master level; fifth dan is considered high master level. Only when one attains the level of high master is he given the status of professional; he has now earned the equivalent of a full masters degree. It takes a completely dedicated person at least seven or eight years of intensive study to attain the junior renshi grade of fourth dan after having trained in the kyu and low dan levels. The Japanese Karatekas who make a renshi grade usually start their training as teenagers, attaining the fourth dan level sometime in their thirties. It of course varies with individual talent, but this is generally the case.

The fourth level grade requires that a Karateman be absolutely committed to developing the art of teaching Karate as a profession. Renshi usually work for a master in a large dojo or work in a small dojo on franchise from their sensei for the years that it takes to become established. They develop leadership through the teaching of others, in this way building the foundation of a reputation. This grade is the proving ground for those who have the talent, dedication, courage, and skill to become a "true sensei." Persons having achieved the grade of renshi are entitled to the honorific name of "sensei" by their juniors when they have become established first-rate professionals.

Mainly through the beneficial propagation of their particular Karate system, Karatekas can achieve the senior grade of fifth dan over a period of about seventeen years. Although some Karate styles terminate at the fifth dan level, in most styles this is only the halfway point for the very few who devote their entire life to the art.

The sixth, seventh, and eighth dan levels are all referred to as the "kyoshi" grade. Literally translated, it means "wizard" or very high master; these levels are commensurate with a Ph.D. The color of the belt is solid black with a red line running through the center. These grades are for the very few who have become wizards in a martial arts system; only outstanding contributors can achieve such distinction.

Other factors in determining one's advancement to this level are many and varied. Certain policies in the system must be considered as well as the personal opinions of the other masters and grand masters and the final evaluation of the chief grand master. One's skill and personal character must be of the highest possible calibre and must have been responsible for the development of thousands of fine Karate students and successful men. Needless to say, one will not see a youthful wizard in a Karate system of great repute.

The head instructor of a true dojo of any traditional system must be established under a franchise within the original Karate system. The local dojo is responsible to the head dojo of the system, which is called the "Honbu Dojo," and must support it financially. The chief grand master or grand patriarch of the system resides and teaches in the "Honbu Dojo." Unfranchised dojos are those of any traditional system which do not contribute a monthly stipend to the support of the head dojo. These dojos are then designated in Japanese as "meechee dojos" (street dojos), and their instructors are called outlaws and treated accordingly by the hierarchy of the system. This has the same effect as a lawyer being disbarred or a doctor being ousted from a medical association.

A solid red belt is worn by the highest grand masters, those who have achieved ninth or tenth dan. The tenth dan, "Ju-Dan" or "Seiko-Sheehan," is the chief grand master; he is the only one in his system. At present there are not more than twelve ninth and tenth dans in all the martial arts systems in the world. Those special men who have reached this highest plateau are above academic equivalents and have attained the status of "most high international grand master" in the martial arts world; they are indeed revered.

Almost all martial arts masters and grand masters belong to a fraternity called the "Butokai," with its headquarters formerly in Kyoto, Japan. Recently the name has been changed to "Budokan" and its location shifted to Tokyo. There is an elaborate and very strict process for the recognition of a master and for his subsequent appointment to the Budokan Board of Governors. One's appointment is finally decided upon by a collective vote of the grand masters of the various martial arts belonging to the organization. At the present time, the chief representative of the Karate division of the Tokyo Budokan is the Seiko-

"It is symbolic of life."

Sheehan (Chief Grand Master) of the Gojuryu system, Professor Gogen Yamaguchi.

It must be remembered by all those who study a martial art that a student's advancement from one level to the next is contingent as much upon his character development as upon his skills. Of course, the basic requirement for progression is faithful execution of the physical skills and techniques of each level, but far more is involved. The central theme of Karatedo, the philosophy that is repeated to

45

the student night after night, is "perpetual self-improvement." Not only is he to work for greater physical health and for greater strength of body, but he must also work to become a better person. Novices in Karate are often surprised to hear that they are expected to read widely, to work toward the development of their minds as well as their bodies. Karatekas are expected to set up goals for themselves and to give their all in working toward realization of those goals. Failure is inexcusable. The realization of one goal must be the father of the next. This is the Karateman's life cycle. The physical fighting of Karate is equivalent to the competition in life; Karate is in fact reality. It is symbolic of life.

Judomen in summer training at the Tokyo Budokan (1966).

One's own iron will

There is no exact equivalent in the English language for the Karate words "chi" or "ki"; for lack of a more precise word, we shall use the terms "focus" or "intrinsic strength."

Focus consists of all the physical, mental, and spiritual energies of a human being brought to bear upon any particular point with all the concentration of which a person is capable. It is a lightning-like unleashing of one's energy with explosive suddenness. Although every human being possesses intrinsic strength, it is rarely used except as the result of severe stress. Thus, accidentally touching a hot stove will cause a person to move his hand with unexpected suddenness; being locked in a burning room will bring out the bulldozer strength required to smash down the door. Karatemen can amass and release this explosive force at will.

"Chi" sustains the same relationship to the Karate weapons of punch and kick that gunpowder bears to a bullet. Its characteristics are evident in training when striking or kicking causes one's uniform sleeve or trouser leg to snap in the air like a snake whip. The degree of audibil-

47

ity indicates the measure of one's chi development; it is impossible to produce a snapping sound without explosive speed. The "one punch man" and the "knock-out punch" are colloquial terms which represent the idea of focus.

The development of chi does not come quickly: it evolves over a long period of time. These energies are not a static force waiting to be released, but are instead considered to be a stream of universal strength and power which motivates all things. It continually flows through one's body from the pelvic region to all the extremities. A person who consciously or unconsciously allows his chi development complete freedom of flow seems to charge the air around him with electricity: the moment such a person enters a room, a dynamic presence is felt, and all eyes turn toward him. The flow of it should never be restricted by inhibitions. When one is conscious of one's chi (not self-conscious, for that would confine it), one is then able to direct its power in any area of endeavor. The benefits of the conscious development of focus are overwhelming, for they can be used in every facet of life.

The term "kiai" (another manifestation of chi) is understood by most beginning Karate students to be the explosive forcing out of the breath in the form of a loud, intensely piercing yell or scream, propelled by the muscles of the lower diaphragm. The scream is released at the exact moment of impact, thus clearing the student's mind of fear and enabling him to commit himself totally to his action. The kiai, when developed to maturity, becomes a weapon in itself. It is reputed to have been used by masters to shock persons at a distance into insensibility, as well as to resuscitate apparently lifeless bodies when accompanied by the proper physical manipulations.

There are two aspects of kiai which are not auditory and which, once experienced, are never forgotten. The first is called "kiai of the eyes," or "cat-eyes power." It is terrifying, for it consists of all the chi development expelled from the eyes. The saying "if looks could kill" originates from this ability; some Karate masters have been known to kill with a look and little else.

The second aspect is known as "the real kiai," for it eventually takes on ultimate importance for all Karatemen. The real kiai consists of unremitting concentration on developing "one's own iron will." Such concentration on will power causes both the mind and the body to develop to the point where one is able to do the seemingly impossible without realizing it.

One's progress in Karate depends upon the intensity with which one devotes himself to constant practice. Fulfilling one's potential as a person can stem only from the real kiai idea in practice and in living; the pride and skill that this kind of consistency brings to a student are motivating forces which feed upon themselves, continually growing stronger. "The real kiai," or "one's own iron will," is what Karatemen meditate on when breaking what seem to be impossible barriers to their punching, striking, or kicking power. It was with this kind of concentration that Chinese Karate masters could kill horses and their armor-covered riders. So great was their efficiency that one barehanded punch to the heart of the horse was fatal. There is a Karate master living in Japan today who, also

Mas. Oyama in Madison Square Garden, November, 1962 .

barehanded, fought and killed a bull without injury to himself. His name is Mas. Oyama. The story of this fight has become a legendary example of chi development and the real kiai.

Development of the iron will begins with the first punch a beginner delivers to the "makiwara" (Karate striking device). Using the makiwara is of utmost importance in the "hard" development (known as "go") of a student's strength of limbs and power. When used in conjunction with proper training routines, the makiwara challenges the punching ability and perpetually refines it. There are many types of such training aids: the orthodox Karate striking post, the heavy or light canvas bag, the very heavy leather punching bag, and even a feather suspended in air by a string are all considered useful in training. The student varies the use and type of his striking device according to the progress of his development until he discovers the one device or combination of training aids that suit him perfectly. New Karate students have the common misconception that their objective is merely to beat their hands on the inanimate object. It takes time before they understand the feeling of hitting the object with developed force via the trained punch and kick. Only time and experience can bring about the understanding of this concept.

Hitting the makiwara is a courage-building device in the first year of training. Not more than one out of every ten Karate students really contacts the makiwara: the rest never understand or believe in it because it seems to be based on too primitive an idea. Its psychological ramifications are manifold. Many Karate teachers have made a personal study of the personalities of their students by observing their reactions to makiwara training: there are significant correlations between the way a student trains in school and the way he is in life. Teachers can analyze their students by observing the way they walk, punch, fight, perform training dances, and react to the group training environment.

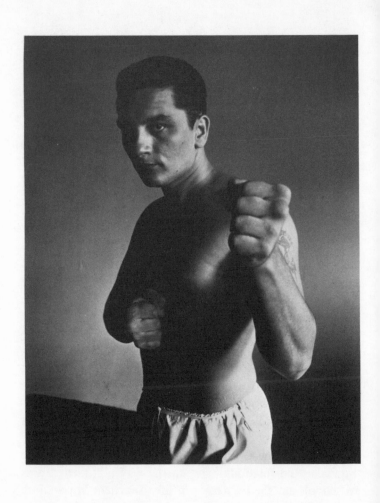

First development (hard aspect), derived from makiwara punching and push-ups on the knuckles.

Students who train seriously eventually realize the importance of the makiwara and build or procure one of their own. Without it they cannot adequately preserve the hard aspect of their style. Dedicated students use the makiwara five days per week for short periods of time. They also use relatively light weights (preferably dumbbells) and do at least fifty repetitions of their favorite exercises. Their regime is flexible, but it can be said that most of them train two-hundred and sixty days each year. Generally, training consists of body-building, followed by makiwara training, ending with dynamic tension kata (motion study) practice of their favorite training dances and zazen (sitting, relaxing, breathing, thought collecting, introspection, and seemingly doing absolutely nothing). The entire health routine consumes approximately twenty minutes per day once understanding is accomplished. This is only their minimum personal routine exclusive of their life in the dojo. They all know that one is in superior mental and physical condition only when one is in regular training.

The student is able to measure his progress in iron will development by means of "tamashowari," the practice of breaking inanimate objects. The purpose is to destroy with one strike a breakable object such as a board, a brick, or a stone; the challenge of tamashowari is to do what others cannot possibly do. The terrific pressure of performing this in public is a true test of the Karateman's iron will, for to fail is unthinkable.

There was a Karate teacher in a recent exhibition at New York City's Hunter College who punched so hard that he broke a brick, the cinder block under the brick, and the

Board breaking for testing strength.

chair holding the cinder block in a single shot. Those who have learned the art of complete commitment suffer neither damage nor pain. One is at his peak in this ability between the ages of twenty and thirty.

Kata and jiu-kumite

A kata is a series of fighting movements combining breathing, striking, and defensive techniques to suit innumerable situations. These fighting movements are manifested in the form of choreography, which allows the student to fully express the four basic tenets of Karate: speed, strength, technique, and beauty. Each kata has a particular rhythmical sequence (without which it would be mere movement) and is designed for the imaginary fighting of several opponents.

The katas are the essence of Karate; without them Karate would be the mere learning of various fighting and self-defense techniques, expressing nothing and allowing for no aesthetic development. Katas are the distilled, concentrated wisdom, understanding, and experience of hundreds of great Karate masters, translated into a language of rhythmical movement, breathing, and peak awareness. When one begins to understand them, one glimpses a new world of untold internal riches.

The primary meaning of the kata is for the performer himself. If he is unable to immerse himself in the kata and so release his emotions, or life force, a master will say of the performer that he is still "in the dance," that is, unable to emote or express his feelings at will. This poignant Karate saying has an even more profound meaning when the sensei refers to a student "coming out of the dance." This is the highest compliment one can receive.

In their formative years in the dojo, Karate students must think in terms of thousands of repetitions, for only constant repetition will enable them to master the basic fighting and defense forms and thus become fine fighters. But not until they become fine kata performers do students have an inkling of what Karate really means and what is meant by the phrase "coming out of the dance."

The eventual perfection of the katas leads not only to mastery of the basic forms, but also to physical and spiritual sensitivity and to complete control of all parts of the body. The forms attain new meanings: they enable a student to meditate while in action—he seems to float above himself, to watch his own performance. It is only at this point in his development that the Karateman begins to sense the movements of his opponents before they occur, thus enabling him to react with blinding speed and absolute clarity and control. Mastering the katas forces the Karate student to the point of "coming out of the dance." When the martial arts student achieves this freedom, he is on the road to the attainment of the bliss and understanding of the masters, for only in dynamic kata performance can one be truly explosive and exact. One can then give free reign to his passion and skill.

Many katas were originated in ancient times by various masters, each master adding his own discoveries to the particular kata that became his favorite. Thus, these dance forms were interpreted, modified, and enriched over the centuries. Others were originated comparatively recently, and still others are even now in the process of creation and modification.

Young students must realize that even the old grand masters practice and meditate on the katas every day of their lives. Only by such dedication have they reached their superb degree of skill and understanding. The renowned professor, Gogen Yamaguchi, exemplifies this spirit of devotion. Through his profound study and understanding of the katas, he has developed an uncanny knowledge of the nature of movement so that, when he is fighting, all forceful moves directed at him seem to be carried along as if on a current of air, the sensei directing them away from himself or against his opponent with effortless will. After seeing a Karateman of such excellence, the serious martial arts student invariably does his best to perfect his katas.

Many beginners in Karate would rather spend all their time fighting than endure the discipline and hard work necessary to perfect the katas of their style. But they soon learn that a fighter who does not know the katas well can go only as far as his physical limits and thus stays "in the dance." A good Karateman first develops his katas to perfection and later perfects his jiu-kumite (sparring) ability. When a Karateman is able to come out of the dance, skill and jiu-kumite come to him naturally.

One of the strongest traditions in Karate is its sense of secrecy. Having originated with the monks of the Shaolin

There are limits to how far a fighter can go, but there are no limits to how far a good Karateman can go!

Monastery, this tradition has always influenced the teaching of Karate, especially regarding the katas. Karatemen tend to be secretive about their important discoveries; they do not want them to be misused or cheapened through easy access. For this and other reasons, many of the movements and postures in the performance of the katas are disguises for the true movements, and many meanings contained within them are varied to contain the mood or intention of the performer.

The Goju Karate style of Japan as well as the Shotokan Karate style place enormous emphasis on the study and mastery of katas. All senseis know that the effort required to master them is the key to self-enlightenment (Satori).

After one has studied the katas for a sufficient length of time, he has the potential to become an outstanding exponent of jiu-kumite. Sparring takes the form of light, yet forceful, highly-controlled and purposeful blows to all the vulnerable areas of one's opponent. The eyes and the genitals, while being the primary targets in one's training for fighting, are never direct targets for contact in sparring. This practice-fighting between Karatemen permits only one fully focused contact blow, called "sweeping," an irregular type of kicking against the opponent's ankle or nerve centers of the knee for the purpose of knocking him to the ground.

Jiu-kumite is ideally a realistic, highly-spirited practice of "shobu," the Japanese term for actual combat. It is the responsibility of each Karateman to defend himself in order to keep from being injured and to control himself in order to prevent injuries to others. Undue hostility and aggression are never tolerated by Karate schools; in a well-controlled dojo, the command "Yame" by the teacher or a senior grade black belter orders the immediate cessation of any attack or action. Such a practice eliminates unnecessary injuries which the more experienced men can foresee. Jewelry or chains about the neck and long finger nails or toe nails provide unnecessary danger and are not acceptable in the dojo.

In most systems, jiu-kumite is practiced on all levels of development including the white belt (beginners) level, but the lower levels are continuously cautioned to keep the focus points comparatively far from the actual target area. It takes a great deal of skill to control one's reactions so closely; this is why in some Karate systems no jiu-kumite is allowed below the black belt level. In certain rough dojos, it used to be fashionable among the students to consider injuries like broken noses and cauliflower ears a mark of distinction until one evening a sensei rebuked them strongly for this attitude, saying that such things were the mark of an unskilled fighter. From that time on, these and similar badges of courage were somewhat sheepishly referred to as "regrettable moments of unskillfulness."

The senior black belters are constantly alert in order to prevent accidents. In an emergency, they immediately apply "katsu," or resuscitation techniques, to the injured fighter. Katsu is a highly specialized first aid; the secret of helping injured fighters lies in the immediacy of the succor.

The most common method of judging in Karate tournaments is the point count system: a given number of skillful strikes to vulnerable areas of the opponent are decided on by a group of experienced Karatemen coordinated by a chief-referee. Although this system has proved itself to be the best practical method of determining winners in contests, many Karatemen dislike it. They claim that it is an unfair method because a fighter who is strong and courageous will often take a blow in order to deliver his own: he is therefore not at his best within the rules of the orthodox point system.

In a contest that is a real fight rather than a sporting event, the most satisfying way to determine the better

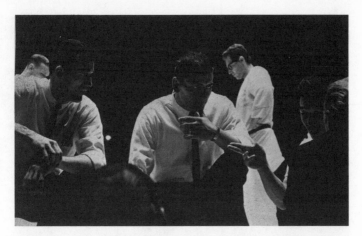

*United Karate Federation masters of New York and New Jersey,
Madison Square Garden, 1962. From left to right: Don Nagle,
Isshando (Okinawa); Peter Urban, Gojuryu (Japan); S. Henry
Cho, Jee-Do-Kwan (Korea).*

fighter is the time system, which incorporates the one or
two minute round as in boxing. The essence of the style is
shown in these fights. Occasionally, masters of different
styles will fight each other in a five minute round with no
judges or referees; a serious student can derive great benefit by watching masters fight.

A jiu-kumite bout, in either a dojo or a tournament, begins with an expression of respect for one's opponent. The
two fighters stand in an attentive position facing each
other. Their sensei stands between them but off to the side,
thus facing them both. Upon the instruction of the sensei

61

"The essence of the style is shown in these fights."

or referee, the fighters assume their fighting stance. Bouts begin and end on the referee's command.

Karate bouts start with an introductory phase. The fighters usually try their feinting techniques and various opening moves in order to determine the reactions and the skills of their opponent. They then begin to use the "in-fighting" techniques: it is here that the fighters' speed and ability at close hand work show. The conclusion comes when one fighter takes the initiative of launching a full, focused attack which results in a definite and overpowering termination of the fight, such as the knocking down of the opponent by a sweep or a series of body and head blows. The better fighter will always be recognized by the timing and pace he uses in "seizing opportunity." He inevitably ends at the right moment. This means "knock-out" effort to Karatemen; a great deal of their experience in the dojo prepares them for this. The final attack must be sudden and fierce, preceded by a complete change of pace. One always avoids telegraphing offense. Only by periodic competition is a high level of morale maintained. Competition keeps the Karate student geared to the art all his life.

Contradictory as it may seem, there is always a winner in a Karate bout, but there is never a loser. Both the stronger and the weaker benefit from such sparring practice; every mistake is a stepping stone. Spectators at Karate schools are often amazed at the way two men will vigorously fight one another and afterwards be the greatest of friends. There are no closer people than Karate students who have given their all in a good fight.

The Goju style

Each system of Karate has its own symbol. The insignia by which the Goju style of Japan is recognized is the clenched hard fist, an example of which is shown as the frontispiece of this book. It was modeled after the right fist of the founder of the Goju style, a master named Chojun Miyagi. He was known to have had fingers strong enough to pierce a side of beef. Chojun Miyagi occasionally did this at Karate exhibitions in the old days to show the strength of a Karate hand form called "nukite," or "spear-hand." This sort of demonstration of Karate power is almost extinct now.

Chojun Miyagi lived in China where he studied Karate for many years. He blended the strong snap techniques of the Okinawan style with the dynamic and free technique of the soft Chinese kenpo. It was thus that the beginning of the highly distinctive Gojuryu Karate system was evolved.

Professor Gogen Yamaguchi was the primary disciple of Miyagi and is now the chief grand master of the Japanese Gojuryu Karate system. He teaches actively every night in the Gojuryu honbu dojo in the Bunkyo-ku section

Gogen Yamaguchi, 10th Dan Patriach of Gojuryu.

In the Tokyo Goju dojo, 1954.

*Chojun Miyagi,
founder of Goju Karate.*

of Tokyo. He has three handsome sons and two beautiful daughters, all of whom have been training in Karate since the age of four. His book, entitled *Goju Karate,* is the official text book of all the principles of Gojuryu Karate— its techniques, philosophy, and breathing.

Yamaguchi sensei has been nicknamed "the cat" by westerners who visit his magnificent school. This is because of his catlike movements and his long, flowing hair. His hair is like the mane of a lion; his eyes are like those of a tiger.

Professor Yamaguchi's synthesis of Karate, Zen, yoga, and Shinto religion evolved into what is called in English "the way of hard and soft." The lion with its power and lightning-like moves is the symbol of the Gojuryu ideal. Karatemen have learned from a study of the big cats much of great value about the art of relaxation and breathing. Goju Karate students train their bodies in the peculiar breathing and dynamic tension exercises that are exactly like the abdominal breathing and stretching movements of the big cats. The breathing in particular is the hallmark of the Goju style. The Karate students who learn it well are able to rejuvenate themselves at will. With proper breathing techniques they can overcome the miseries of colds and sickness and make any part of their body impervious to pain.

The Goju style specializes in close in-fighting techniques. The breathing system provides the ability to take a blow while enabling the student to deliver the most powerful of blows. There are now several dojos in America where this style is taught.

Sensei Yamaguchi at home in his dojo.

The chief grand master in the mountains.

Special Zen training with Professor Yamaguchi.

We who are studying Karate do aspire to these virtues:
1. We are proud to study the spirit of Goju.
2. We shall practice courtesy.
3. We shall be quick to seize opportunity.
4. We shall always practice patience.
5. We shall always keep the fighting spirit of Karate.

Potential and goals

*T*he great hope of American Karate teachers is that Karate will soon become a vital part of the nation's police training. It would be a truly progressive move for metropolitan cities. Although many academies have begun to experiment with Karate, the obstacles to full implementation of such a program are enormous. Conservative officials are hesitant to allocate the necessary funds and revise the present system. Their attitude is understandable, for, until recently, little was known about Karate. It is probable that, as the public becomes increasingly enlightened about Karate, so too will the police academies, and they will act accordingly.

In Japan almost every police precinct has its own dojo where its men train in the various martial arts, for it is believed that a good policeman must be a good physical fighter. Oriental policemen use their Karate ability before they use their club, hand cuffs, or gun. In Japan and China, the officers have no physical fear of doing their jobs. They are not only respected as law officers, but also feared as exceptionally capable bare-handed fighters. There are absolutely no instances in the Orient where hoodlums may feel superior to policemen as fighters. Even young rookie policemen patrol their areas in a high crime-rate section with great authority and confidence. The precinct dojo keeps them in the peak of physical and mental condition throughout their entire careers. In American police academies, proficiency in Karate could become a reflection of the physical fitness of each academy graduate. The achievement of fighting excellence would be an incentive to keep them climbing the ladder of success in their career. A policeman's bare-handed fighting ability should be as important to him as his side arm.

The militaristic structure of a Karate dojo and the demands of discipline and physical effort are all conducive to the structure of a law enforcement agency. Competent policemen will eventually realize this. With the martial arts developing in America the way they are now, this might well happen within the next two decades. It is also predicted that someday Karate will become a part of the physical education system of our military academies. This would be one of the greatest achievements possible for Karate propagation in our country. Academy graduates with a four year program of Karate training behind them would be ideal military officers. Over the past ten years, generals of the American armed services have seen the value of a martial arts program for its men; they invariably notice that it causes a great esprit de corps.

It would naturally occur that only the goshin jitsu (self-defense) aspects of Karate would be adopted by a law enforcement agency preparing to use Karate. It would be sufficient for their uses, because the simple levels needed

74

American Karatemen at the Chinese YMCA of San Francisco.

for practical effectiveness could be attained in a reasonable period of time with a few training periods per week.

As Karate continues to attract the attention of many peoples throughout the world, it will foster grand championships that will link distant lands. It will inevitably become a major cultural exchange between the United States and Japan.

In the beginning years of the spread of the martial arts outside of Japan most people were so impressed with the little they saw that they judged it to be the whole thing.

Karate, the weaponless weapon!

But they only witnessed the physical aspects; the fighting techniques alone were so impressive that they were emulated by many and considered to be the essence of Karate. This is why misunderstanding, misrepresentation, and crass commercialism were possible in the early years of judo and jiu-jitsu propagation in America.

A Karateman in training is in Karate
Strength comes from health.
Speed comes from effort.
Technique comes from experience.
Will power comes from faith.
Serenity comes from old knowledge.
Progress comes from new knowledge.

Guideline for self-analysis

Individual Karatemen are a composite picture of the below listed characteristics. The object of the true Karateman is to achieve as many Class "A" characteristics as possible.

A	B	C
Harmonizes hard and soft	Separates hard and soft	Knows no soft
Efficient	Compulsive	Restricted
Tournament fighter	Won't get involved	Is afraid of competition
Quick to seize opportunity	Wastes time	Has no patience
Corrects errors	Rationalizes	Doesn't know difference
Lives Karate daily	Part-time person	Will drop Karate too
Looks, acts, and feels sharp	Only when in the mood	Has no feelings
Lives in reality	Relies on others	Is disoriented
Knows nothing is free	Practices false economy	Loves poverty
Blocks soft, hits hard	Overcompensates with feet	Can't experience anger
Self-controlled	Loses control	Will fold in jiu-kumite
Knows self	Magnifies self	Underestimates others
Works for a better life	Lives for a better work	Is afraid of work
Never breaks training	Has no future	Has no faith
Learns from everything	Doesn't listen to others	Will not read
Seeks happiness from inside	Seeks happiness outwardly	Waits for happiness
Relies on self	His word means nothing	Has no friends
Gets better with age	Gets weaker with age	Gets smaller with age

Class "A" Lightweights

Speed and endurance
Big threat at close quarters with elbows and knees
Likes to hit and run
Utilizes circular motion
Develops many combinations
Attacks in bursts
Perfects jumping backhand
Will wear opponent down
Operates well in cat stance
Never skips makiwara
Fights viciously
Most spectacular style
Builds defined muscles, powerful calves and forearms
Never skips meals
Never dissipates

Class "A" Middleweights

Versatility and long range
Attacks face with jump kicks and round kicks
Likes to dance and sharpshoot
Will harrass, sweep and trip
Perfects back kick
Dances and feints
Perfects lunge punch
Will suddenly change pace
Operates well in horse stance
Never skips kata
Fights relentlessly
Most interesting style
Builds elongated muscles, broad shoulders and flat gut
Keeps balanced diet
Always exercises

Class "A" Heavyweights

One punch knockout power
Always ends fight at close quarters
Likes to grab and hit
Will slug it out
Develops big kiai power
Stalks
Perfects blocking systems
Will study opponent first
Operates well in sanchin
Never skips jogging
Fights ruthlessly
Most popular style
Builds massive chest, big fists, and strong feet
Aware of rest and nutrition
Puts health first

Rigorous discipline and group competition work for the further-ance of physical health and strength of character.

Famous dojo stories

Researching the history of the martial arts is in the final analysis a matter of accumulating, cross-checking, and listening to the varied accounts of the best of the living Oriental scholars and the great practitioners. It cannot realistically be determined when any of these arts began or by whom. It is generally accepted by Karate devotees that Bodhidharma started the original martial arts concept with the propagation of his Zen sect into China and, through Zen Buddhism, into Japan. But no one can state unequivocally that this is a fact, for, although ancient Chinese and Japanese documents regarding the martial arts do exist, they contradict each other. The general practice of martial arts scholars is to accept as most authentic the opinions of the most erudite and intellectually superior individuals only because their guesses are more educated; however, all scholars, no matter how erudite, preface their findings with an apology for their lack of responsibility for historical accuracy.

The following collection of stories represents the history of Karate as I envision it, having gleaned what seems to me to be most feasible from the massive amounts of contradictory material written on the subject. I have found from my brief experience of only fifteen and a half years of formal practice and research that nothing is impossible in the martial arts, and I therefore take the liberty to depict the past as I believe it was or might well have been. I do not choose to argue with the greater Oriental scholars in the event of disputes with my opinions, but will bow to them on the premise that my guesses are based on less experience than theirs.

However, I believe my findings to be more profound than all the tales and myths about Karate that have been handed down to martial arts devotees for generations. I am basing my conclusions on an admixture of intimate experience, creative imagination, free observation, personal reason, and logic. I have written this book in accordance with the view that sometimes it is better to tell the truth in the guise of stories so as to offend the fewest people, and entertain the most readers. Also, I hope to inform the few who do not need academic accreditation and the dictates of others to help them to decide what is true, what is not true, what is good, what is not good.

The Shaolin Monastery

At some time during the sixth century, the Buddhist monk Bodhidharma, who is generally acknowledged to be the original propagator of the martial arts concept, traveled from India to China for two purposes: to found a Buddhist monastery and to unite the various Buddhist and Taoist schools of thought which had sprung up in China. The undertaking of such a journey even today, with guides, motorized transport, pack animals, firearms, and the other paraphernalia considered necessary for an exploratory expedition, is an enormous and extremely dangerous task requiring months of planning and logistics. The difficulties Bodhidharma faced must have seemed insurmountable to an ordinary man. Consider some of them: the Himalaya Mountains, the highest, coldest, and most forbidding terrain in the world; a country teeming with wild animals and even wilder people, who robbed and killed travelers as a matter of course; the distance itself, a matter of some two thousand five hundred miles as the crow flies, but in reality probably three times that distance; no roads and in many places not so much as a foot path; no maps or guides; and even Bodhidharma's religion, which forbade him to carry weapons.

Alone, on foot, and unarmed, Bodhidharma successfully completed his journey, probably the first man to cross the Himalaya Mountains. When he arrived at Honan province, he immediately founded the Shaolin Monastery. Even to this day, a veil of secrecy surrounds the mysteries of its creation and structure.

At first there was nothing—except Bodhidharma. Doubtless he alone built the first shelter out of whatever materials he could find, using them simply, usefully, beautifully. Gradually, the number of his disciples increased until there was enough manpower to begin erecting the building. This was no ordinary building task, for the standards Bodhidharma imposed on his followers were unprecedented. His demands were so rigorous that the disciples found themselves prostrate from exhaustion time and time again.

Drawing upon the knowledge and experience he had gained from his fabled journey across the mountains, Bodhidharma developed a physical, mental, and spiritual discipline which later came to be known as Zen Buddhism. He knew that, if properly developed, the human body could be a far more diversified and effective instrument than any weapon and that, if this development were coordinated with certain yoga breathing exercises and proper diet, his disciples would attain perfect physical health and stamina. The lawlessness of the times would no longer be a threat to the monks, for their excellent physical condition would render them deadly fighters.

Synthesizing his knowledge of the human body's potential for development with his knowledge of animal fighting techniques, Bodhidharma created a unique system of physical conditioning, weaponless fighting, and mental concentration. His breathing and relaxation techniques came from his study of animals, especially the big cats. The spontaneous explosion of life force, known as "chi," developed from close observation of many animals. He invented many defense and striking techniques by watching insects, reptiles, bears and dogs. The deceptive calm of the sea, which can become a tidal wave; the light touch of a summer's breeze, which can become a typhoon or a cyclone; the immovability and imperviousness to pain of the rocks—all were useful to Bodhidharma. Nothing was neglected.

Through the crystallization of his knowledge, which eventually came to be the Shaolin system, the monks survived and flourished. Although they were religious men, wishing to harm no one and carrying no weapons, they would kill their attackers without a qualm, for they believed that such people were "inhuman humans" and were to be dealt with on their own terms. These monks developed into such formidable fighters that in time they became immune to all danger. Their daily exercise, meditation, and diet enabled them to live to ages that would seem impossible today.

With nothing more than their powerful bodies, the skill and dexterity learned from their technique of fighting movement, and their concentrated will power, the monks gradually created one of the most mysteriously beautiful buildings known to mankind.

There was a solemn symbolism associated with the entrances to the monastery. Although there were three sets of doors—front, side, and rear—everyone, no matter how high his attainments, had to enter through the rear gate: this was unalterable procedure. If a monk could not comply with the disciplines and standards of monastic life, he left through the rear gate, never to return. Those monks who had the intrinsic ability to succeed, but who chose to leave the monastic life, were permitted the honorable use of the side gate. The front gate was used so seldom that the monks measured the passage of time by the rare occurences of its use. It was reserved exclusively for those who had successfully completed the examination for a certified master of the North Shaolin fighting system. Because of the finality of success or failure, few undertook the trial of the examination.

For people far removed from the disciplinary demands of this kind of life, it is difficult to imagine the amount of time and the intense effort required in training. To be deemed worthy of undergoing this examination, one would train for at least twenty years. The test was an experience unique unto itself. As far as we know today, the candidate received neither instructions nor hints as to what he would encounter.

One was led through the monastery cellars to a labyrinth built far beneath. Once he was inside, the doors would be closed and sealed, preventing retreat. The candidate knew that there was only one way out: his fate would be either triumph or death. The labyrinth, which was divided into two chambers, was cold and damp; the walls oozed moisture and were slimy to the touch. Rats, spiders, and reptiles brushed against, clung to, and scurried around the candidate. There was almost total darkness; there were pits that had to be instinctively avoided, for one false step would be injurious if not fatal. Arrows and spears shot out from concealed hiding places in the walls. Stones and axes fell without warning and had to be dodged or caught. Eerie shadows danced in the shallow light which fell on the skeletons of former, unfortunate candidates, who now served as ghastly inspirations.

The labyrinth narrowed so much in places that it seemed impossible to proceed, being less than twelve inches wide. But the candidate had been taught that nothing was impossible. If he could prevent fear from trapping him, he would be able to find a way out. After much time had passed, the exhausted yet alert candidate saw a light in the distance. Instinctively realizing that he was approaching the end of his ordeal, he moved on, not allowing himself to fix his gaze upon the light. He knew that its hypnotic effect would distract his senses from alertness to possible dangers that lay in wait between him and the distant chamber. He inched his way closer.

At last he approached the room, golden with the light of candles. His eyes quickly adjusted to the brilliance and focused on objects which were hanging on the walls. Weapons! The choice ranged from spears, knives, and hatchets to clubs, chains, and bows and arrows of all sizes and shapes. Some served a single purpose; others were more flexible in their use. Why were they needed? What was behind the next door? Some lettering on the wall instructed,

"Choose only one." The candidate knew that he dared not wait; the longer the wait, the more difficult the decision. He could not risk confusion. Relying upon his instinct and reasoning, he noticed that one instrument was different from the others. Yes, the golden shovel was undoubtedly the proper choice. Quickly he seized it from the wall and entered the next room. The door closed. In the Stygian darkness, the candidate sensed that the room was alive with crawling things. He realized immediately what they must be and why he had instinctively chosen the shovel; the crawling things were scorpions, thousands of them, covering the walls, ceiling, and floor, crawling over one another. In this split second, the scorpions had already dropped to his clothing. He violently shook them off and shoveled them away, beginning to clear a path across the room. He smashed them with the back of the shovel, buried them in the sand, hit them in mid-air. It was a continual circular movement of smash, shovel, swing, shovel, smash. He was completely surrounded but did not stop to judge his damage or evaluate the odds against his success. Just before reaching the far door, he realized the difficulty of opening it. His decision was instantaneous; with a constant, sweeping, circular movement of the shovel held in one hand, he pulled back the door with the other and entered the next chamber. Again the door closed behind him, leaving him in total darkness.

He sensed that he was in an enormous, empty, stone-walled chamber. Quickly his strong, sensitive fingers, glided over the walls, seeking the slight indication of another door. So cunningly were the walls constructed that he could find nothing, not even the door he had just passed through. What could this mean? A flash of intuitive understanding answered his question; this was to be the final test. Somehow he must find the way out, using every resource at his command. His breathing deepened, slowed, almost stopped. Suddenly he knew. His heightened sensitivity had felt the tiniest possible movement of air, less than that needed to move a wisp of smoke.

High, high up on one wall were two small openings, roughly a shoulder length apart, large enough to admit the passage of a man's hands and arms. This must be the key. Deliberately he measured off the length of the floor from one wall to the opposite. Standing there, he realized that all he possessed in the way of "chi" must be released now, and that once this attainment was reached, he must never let go.

With the suddenness of a bullet, he shot across the floor and, with an explosive scream that seemed to shatter the very stones themselves, he leaped, scrambled, clawed, willed his way to the top of the wall, found the holes, and thrust his arms in as far as his shoulders.

He found himself hugging a metal object similar to an enormous vase. At the same time, he became aware of the odor of burning flesh, and he realized that the inside of his forearms were resting on white hot metal. With the last of his strength, concentration, and will, he forced himself to hold on. As he did so, he felt the wall on which he was transfixed begin to turn, as though on a pivot. Slowly the vast stone door revolved on its axis until, with a shock of recognition, the candidate found himself deposited not only outside the labyrinth, but outside the monastery as well.

The test was over. He had left by the front gate. He was a certified master of the Shaolin Monastery, and on his forearms was his diploma—two dragons deeply branded into the flesh.

The Okinawan champion

From the time of the Japanese conquest of Okinawa, in the seventeenth century, the Imperial forces had to contend with an extremely self-reliant, fierce, and proud people. Their hostile stubbornness would not allow anyone to break their spirit, even though the Japanese, through superior numbers, armor, and swordsmanship had conquered their homeland.

By means of guerrilla warfare, the Okinawans were able to harrass the Japanese troops; due to the distance between Japan and Okinawa, the occupying forces had great difficulty in continuously replacing their materials and their steadily depleting forces. In an effort to strengthen their position and subjugate the Okinawans, the Japanese ordered the confiscation of all metals on the island. This meant all weapons, tools, cutlery, and every source of replacement, including cooking pots and pans. All forges were dismantled and removed. The Okinawans were disarmed; possession of any weapon was forbidden. The Japanese now thought that they had eliminated the strength of the opposition and that their task would be considerably easier. It was—but only for a short time.

The confiscation of metal caused many problems for the Okinawans. As fighters they felt very insecure without their weapons. Also, unlike the Japanese, they were primarily meat eaters and could not butcher their animals. It was difficult to prepare their food and do their work efficiently without proper instruments. They endured these hardships for a while, but their will to resist gradually strengthened, and they finally formed a delegation to present their grievances to the Imperial forces.

The Japanese commander recognized not only the validity of the complaint, but the possible consequences if he did not compromise. He knew that the success of any occupation is largely dependent on the continuation of the occupied people's habits and ordinary functioning. It was necessary that he make some allowances that would benefit the Okinawans and at the same time enforce the original mandate. It was decided that each village would have a community knife which would be kept in an open square attached to a heavy anchored chain and which would be guarded by two Japanese soldiers. This plan seemed to prove satisfactory. Since the trouble had apparently ceased, the occupying forces began to relax their guard.

But the Okinawans did not relax. Among the old patriarchs there was discussion of old stories remembered from their youth. Some of their people had been to China and had brought back information and stories about the incredible unarmed fighters in Cathay, who were able to defeat armed and armored opponents with nothing but their hands and feet and occasionally with the use of unusual wooden fighting instruments.

After lengthy conferences, the best Okinawan fighters were selected and sent to China to learn the Chinese methods. They were to bring the knowledge home and were given authority to offer high salaries for the importation of teachers. When this was accomplished, the Okinawans began training and started fashioning the wooden instruments. In order to carve them, the trained Karate fighters killed the guards and stole the village knives.

The Karate training was kept completely secret and was guarded against informers. Anyone suspected of being a traitor was kidnapped at night and taken in a boat with a small pig or goat about a mile off shore. There the animal's throat was slit, and it was thrown overboard. When the sharks arrived, the informer invariably lost his balance and fell into the water. It was an infallible security system.

The Japanese never discovered who the teachers were or where the students practiced. The growing resistance was almost imperceptible. Gradually, more and more guards were found dead. Their weapons were gone. The chains and knives would disappear. The impossible was being done, day by day, month by month, year by year. The reports of the military reflected a steadily growing number of murdered sentries. The islanders were developing the Chinese art to the point where their hands and feet were as good as swords for killing other men. The centrifugal force sticks ("neunchaku" and "tunfa") could smash to pieces military armor and the men wearing it. "Okinawa-te" (Okinawan hands) became a consuming terror, a psychological trauma which did not end until the advent of modern firearms in the hands of all occupation troops.

"A giant of seven feet four inches, he had hands and feet that looked like monstrous hams."

By 1915, the days of the Karate warriors seemed over. The art had come, developed, and waned. But that was not the end of it by any means. Only when it became obsolete in war did its true greatness begin. It was a rebirth.

In 1917 the Japanese association of martial arts masters, known as the Butokai, was sufficiently interested in Karate to invite the Okinawans to select their best Karate exponent to visit them. They intended to match this man against their jiu-jitsu masters and thus compare the two fighting systems. This news created widespread excitement on the island.

The peasants felt that Choku Matobu, whose family were also peasant farmers, was the greatest living barehanded fighter. They believed that he was a living legend in his time. He came from an old Karate family famous for having fought the Japanese in many battles in classic Karate manner. But Matobu's reputation came not so much from his finesse as a Karate master as from his unusual physique and phenomenal strength, developed during the years of farm labor when he was a boy. A giant of seven feet four inches, he had hands and feet that looked like monstrous hams. Although he was uneducated and lacked shrewdness, he took full advantage of his brute power and the psychological effect caused by his image. His favorite stance was one called "naihancheen" (the horse), in which he moved as little as possible, choosing to take a series of blows in order to deliver his phenomenal power across the heads of his opponents. He was not a dancer; he preferred to grab his enemies and chop them to death. It was almost impossible to hurt him.

"He proclaimed himself eleventh dan and the greatest warrior on this planet."

Many patriots on the island therefore thought that Matobu would be the one to visit Japan. But he was not chosen for many reasons. He was too unique a character to undertake the venture; in fact, he was insane when he died. He proclaimed himself eleventh dan and the greatest warrior on this planet. He did not speak well, he was not polite, he did not know how to dress, he did not know how to comb his hair, he ate with his hands. He didn't drink tea from tiny cups. He didn't bow or kneel to Japanese people under any conditions. He did not know what it was to take an order or to be told to wait for something. The Japanese would probably have had to shoot him down if an incident had taken place. His temperament prevented his selection.

Among the schools in Okinawa which taught Japanese reading and writing, there was a certain preparatory school for Okinawans who wanted to qualify for Japanese Civil Service. The school, called "Shoto Gakko," taught customs, manners, social graces, all the things necessary for success in the Japanese milieu.

The professor of this institution was an Okinawan of genius. He was astute in all things Japanese and could emulate the Japanese in every way. His manners and speech were impeccable and he wore fine Japanese clothing. He commanded the utmost respect from the well-educated Japanese gentlemen. His name was Gichin Funakoshi.

Although Professor Funakoshi was a brilliant language professor, his all-consuming interest was Karate. He was small only in size; his mind and his courage were limitless. Gichin Funakoshi was friendly with the original propagators of the different styles of Karate in Japan, such as Miyagi Chojun and Gogen Yamaguchi.

It was clear he should go to Japan to represent the Karate of Okinawa, for he fit the need perfectly. The high-ranking Karate masters unanimously agreed that the little professor would go as a fifth dan to inform the Japanese jiu-jitsu masters about Karate!

Arrangements were made, and Funakoshi was off to Japan. What he did there made history in the Japanese martial arts world for he flabbergasted the masters of the Butokai. The little professor, so modest, and "only a fifth dan," defeated every fighter he was matched against, often defeating his opponents with the superior techniques of their own style. He introduced two memorable techniques which subsequently became standard Judo forms: the Judo throw commonly called "uchimata" and the dumping technique referred to as "o-soto-gari." They were originally Karate forms and were, of course, much more deadly in the original.

Because of his affinity to Japanese culture and the respect he won in Japan, Professor Funakoshi felt very much at home during his stay and decided to remain. He had attracted quite a few students with his magnificent performance in the exhibitions, and he began teaching Karate in a Kendo dojo.

It was extremely difficult in the beginning to make Karate understandable to the jiu-jitsu and Kendo conditioned public. There were many excellent would-be Karate students who shied away from it in the early years primarily because it was foreign, and therefore distasteful,

98

according to the mentality of the times. A great Karate professor at one time observed that even the clothes of the Japanese obstructed kicking and punching movements. Their open-toed wooden shoes (geta) and their long-sleeved garments with constricting robes hindered long strides, wide stances, and sudden jumping movements. For this reason the Samurai warriors had developed a method of arranging their clothing to accommodate the particular technique they were using. They did this as casually as if they were in front of their own mirror, while actually fighting for their lives in the heat of a battle. The Chinese, on the other hand, had shoes that looked like sneakers and baggy loose fitting trousers which facilitated all sorts of movements and kicks. Their dress allowed them to punch and use their hands freely. The Okinawans were too poor for fine constricting clothing and consequently were also at home with any type of movement.

Through his superior teaching, Gichin Funakoshi did eventually transcend the barriers of misunderstanding and prejudice against Karate. He was treated with the highest possible respect and was soon able to establish his school as a separate dojo, which he called the "Shoto-kan" after the name of his polishing school in Okinawa. The term "Shoto-kan" now identifies Funakoshi's unique Karate style.

He eventually married a Japanese girl and had two sons. One, Gikko, became a famous Karate master but never reached the heights of his beloved father.

The ninjitsu people

In the olden days there was a strange group of men and women who always dressed in black. The black clothing covered even their faces, and their feet were cushioned in the softest of black felt. They walked in silence and lived at night. They had no friends, for they were universally feared and hated. Many people considered them magicians of the black arts, in league with all that was evil. These "black knights" of the old days, who did not believe in magic themselves but who could perform seemingly magical feats, were the professional assassins of feudal Japan. They were known as "ninja," or "nin-jitsu people."

They devoted their childhood to training for mastery in their peculiar skills and thus were highly skilled in the martial arts. Raised utterly without morals, which they referred to as "imaginary restrictions," they were bereft of virtue.

Since they thrived on darkness, their training halls were painted completely black; varying lengths of nails and spikes protruded from the walls. Upon these spikes and stone walls, they practiced jumping, grasping, climbing, and wall-scaling techniques. They were superb masters of sword-handling, archery, horsemanship, jiu-jitsu, stick fighting, body balancing, and the art of throwing tiny poisoned darts and the small, sharp-cornered coins of that era. This last was a favorite weapon, for who would believe it possible to put out a man's eye and kill him at a distance of more than fifty feet by throwing a coin the size of a silver dollar? No weapon could ever be found—just an ordinary coin lying in the street.

Hundreds of hours were spent practicing walking across creaky wooden floors without making a sound. This was done by unwinding their long, black, felt waistband; rolling it across the floor; carefully, lightly, and quickly darting down its entire length; then rolling it up and repeating the maneuver until the desired distance was crossed. They did everything with their own inimitable magic and called it "ninjitsu," the art of stealth.

Their training, being supremely realistic, also took into consideration every adverse situation they could imagine.

They were the original practitioners of the "art of programming." They were taught from the cradle that nothing was impossible. Not knowing that a thing could not be done, they proceeded to do it.

They had many services to sell to the lords and ladies of the great houses of the day, their specialty being murder and terror. Many provincial lords, in rivalry for one reason or another, often used the ninja in preference to the expense of an all-out war against an enemy. A ninjitsu man could sneak past guards, fool alert watchdogs, do his job, and leave no traces.

They used black coal dust and chemically-produced smoke screens to distort the sight of pursuers. Their visual memory and sense of direction was so exact that, with one swift glance, they could evaluate all means of egress from a building. This enabled them to leap from any second or third story window, knowing in advance that a tree would be underneath to break their fall. Rooftops were nothing but stepping stones to be adroitly traveled upon. Using their uniquely fashioned silken rope and grappling hooks, they scaled the highest, most forbidding cliffs and walls. A skilled ninjitsu man could run down a hallway, jump across the entrance area, grasp the eaves to a doorway, and pull himself up and over onto the roof in a matter of seconds. From the roof, where he blended into the night, he was in a perfect position for throwing darts, coins, or circular dirks that looked like the blades of a power saw. No wonder everyone was afraid of them. Chasing them was almost certain death, for they would seem to disappear right in front of a pursuer's eyes; the next thing the pursuer felt would be the sting of a poisoned dart in the back of his neck.

Occasionally, a ninjitsu man was discovered and captured, but rarely for very long; they had mastered the arts of disappearing and escape as surely as the art of murder. Even when stripped down to nothing but their "fundoshi," or loincloths, they almost always managed to escape. When the guards led a ninjitsu man out to be executed (a foregone conclusion), he would wait until they were outside and surrounded by a very high wall, too high for even him to scale unaided. Suddenly casting off his bonds (for the knot was never invented that could hold them for more than a few minutes), he would completely confound his captors by running full tilt toward the seemingly impregnable wall. Just before he did so, he had urinated into his fundoshi. Removing the sopping wet cotton cloth, he ran up the wall as far as he could, letting out a piercing scream and slapping the wet cloth with all his strength against the top of the stone wall. Without stopping his momentum for an instant, he would swing the remaining distance to the top of the wall, using the cloth as a rope, and, before the astonished and terrified guards could move, he had disappeared.

The mystique of these almost legendary professional assassins increased as the centuries went by. The secrets were handed down from family to family, generation after generation. Some say that even today the ninja exist, but this is not officially certain or admitted. All that is known is that there are a few old martial arts teachers in southern Japan who, for the sake of tradition, still practice the ninjitsu training. These old senseis occasionally give an exhibition of the dying art at the more important martial arts events. They are always looked upon a little fearfully by the younger participants in the exhibition, for after all, who knows?

The Aikido man

A martial arts dojo which is conducted in the spirit of the old Oriental standards of excellence does not advertise itself. It depends only upon its reputation; the higher the calibre of the martial arts men it produces, the greater is its fame. The chief method used by dojos to spread their reputation is to exhibit before large audiences the skills developed by its students.

There once was a great Aikido sensei in Honolulu who brought fame to his dojo by performing sensational feats of speed. No one else in the world would attempt his specialty. He would lean against a wall at a sixty degree angle as if being held in a frisking posture used by Honolulu police. This position required that his body be supported by only one foot, as the toes of his other foot were behind the ankle of his supporting foot. The hands were held high. A skilled policeman could frisk prisoners in such a position and easily sweep them off their feet if they moved. The sensei would then have a police officer press a loaded gun against his back; the officer would count aloud to three and suddenly fire the pistol until all the cartridges were spent.

The sensei, spinning around clockwise from his position fast enough to avoid being shot in the spine, would end in a position directly behind the policeman before the second shot was even fired. This was a most impressive feat, for bullet holes in the wall were clearly visible to the spectators. The fastest trigger finger was no match for the fastest Aikido man.

The students of this Honolulu master were especially skilled in handling wooden swords which they called "bokken." The black belters would often lie hidden in wait for a dojo brother and would suddenly attack him with a bokken when he entered the school. Years of practicing this technique had brought the skilled students to the point where they could perceive a blow before it was delivered, and they would successfully throw the attacker to his back every time. If the victim failed to perceive the approaching attack, he would suffer a painful blow; after experiencing several of these blows, a student usually forced himself to become faster and more precise in his technique and thus was eventually able to halt every attacker. It is such a training attitude which produces the best results in the martial arts schools.

The Japanese magician

The Oriental cultures have long been noted for their preference for the human mind and spirit over the efficiency and reliability of the machine. Perhaps it was with this point of view that the Tokyo police once retained a Karate master on their staff to serve as a "lie detector." It was his task to listen to the interrogation of suspects and tell, simply from listening and watching their facial expressions, characteristics, and mannerisms, whether they were speaking truths or untruths. The police officials valued his opinions highly and worked on his suggestions. Over a period of many years, it was found that not even once was the Karate master wrong in his evaluations.

The Japanese government eventually asked this Karate master to go to Manchuria on a delicate political mission. He accepted, but while he was there he was arrested by the hostile Chinese government and was interned as a political prisoner.

In prison he was treated very badly. Although his jailers did not know who he was, they were afraid of him. They had nothing to base this feeling on, for he was a model prisoner, but for some reason they all felt that he was different—and potentially dangerous.

Unlike most prisoners, he refused to succumb to apathy and inactivity; he trained in Karate every day, alone in his cell, keeping himself healthy in spite of the worst conditions. Since he communicated with no one and could often be found in trance like meditation, some of the more superstitious guards believed him to be a magician.

Eventually his identity became known to the officials of the prison, who thereupon issued orders that he must at all costs be broken down. If successful, it would be a great feather in their cap and a great loss of face for the Japanese to prove the vaunted self-control and strength of Japanese Karate to be mere myth.

They were not successful.

The sensei was placed in solitary confinement, in total darkness. He was given just enough food to sustain life. He was forced to undergo torture, and the Chinese have developed torture to a fine art. None of this affected him. Placing himself in a trance by means of meditation and breathing, he felt neither pain nor emotion nor hunger. He completely confounded his captors and caused even the prison's hardened guards to look upon him with awe.

Finally, the prison officials decided upon a supreme test. After much effort and trouble, they managed to procure a tiger. To be sure, it was not a Bengal tiger in the prime of health, but none-the-less a tiger. They placed the animal in a cage and kept it hungry for three days. The plan was to thrust the Japanese Karate master into the cage, completely naked. If he were in a trance and could feel nothing, he would be killed and eaten. Then the Chinese could charge him with cowardice, saying that he was afraid to die fighting, an unthinkable act for a samurai or martial arts man.

The plan was carried out. They thrust him into the cage with the tiger, apparently at the mercy of a certain fate.

In Karate, nothing is impossible.

The moment he entered the cage, the Karate master seemed possessed. With a terrifying roar, he attacked the tiger! Almost before anyone could realize what had happened, he had kicked the tiger's nose, disorienting the animal, and then had smashed his elbow across the ear of the cat as he dove on its body before it could recover from the initial shock. The Japanese magician, as he was later called by his captors, then embraced the huge cat from behind its neck, applying a reverse arm-bar choke. He tightened every muscle in his body and let out an intense, shattering scream right into the ear of the animal as he strangled it with all his strength and willpower. The tiger died of oxygen starvation in less than twenty seconds.

The spectators were terrified as they gazed upon this man. He looked almost like the incarnation of a tiger himself, and they were convinced that he was not human, that he was possessed by the devil. The witnesses all claimed that he entered the cage with no fear and that in fact the tiger seemed afraid of the man.

Everyone in the political camp was deathly afraid to go near the captured Japanese gentleman, and all breathed a sigh of relief when he was finally released.

His name is Gogen Yamaguchi. Once every year to this

day a group of men, all former prisoners in Manchuria, gather with him and eat brown bread and drink plain water, for this was their diet for over two years. They do this as a reunion to remember the past, appreciate the present, and give thanks to their Shinto God for the future.

The three sons

*I*n the olden days there was a very famous grand master of the sword who was greatly pleased to receive a visit from another old gentleman of his art. As the two senseis, chatting and sipping tea, recalled their youth and valiant deeds, the conversation gradually centered on their respective families and the progress of their children. The host had three sons who had naturally devoted their lives to the task of mastering the sword, as had their father and his father, and his father before him. Greatly desiring to display his sons' skills, and at the same time wishing to teach them a lesson, the father winked mirthfully at his guest. With the stealth of a cat, he took a heavy vase from an alcove in the wall and placed it above the opening corner of the sliding doors that were the entrance to the room. The vase was in such a position that, should the door be opened, the piece of ceramic art would topple onto the head of the person entering.

With twinkling eyes, the two wise patriarchs returned to their tea and talk, for they were patient and had many things to discuss. After quite a while, the grand master called out for his eldest son. As was his nature, the number one son was quick to hear his father's call and came swiftly and gracefully to the door. There was an almost imperceptible pause. The son smoothly pulled the door open to his right, at the same time reaching through and up with his open left hand. Grasping the heavy vase before it had time to fall, he spun clockwise into the room, holding the vase above his head. With a beautiful gesture, he slid the door shut and replaced the vase in its original position above the door. Then, without a word or glance, he bowed humbly to the two old masters.

The father's face beamed as he performed the introductions, saying, "This is my eldest son." His old friend looked deep into the son's eyes for a long moment. Then, with a big smile and a low bow to the father, he replied, "I am very happy for you. He has learned everything well and is mastering the sword. He is worthy of your name." At this, both the father and son bowed in return, and there were tears in the eyes of the grand master, for he knew that his old friend had just accepted his son as a young master of the sword.

After a short time, the father again called out, this time for his second son, who was also quick to respond. He came to the door and immediately opened it. Out of the corner of his eye, he glimpsed the falling vase, and his action was swift and conclusive: nimbly and smoothly he leaped to one side, catching the vase in his arms. His startled eyes glanced around the room, questioning everyone and everything. Politely suppressing his instinct to cry out or ask about the vase, he turned to the door, shut it, and, after a moment of fumbling, managed to replace the vase in its original position. Bows were exchanged, whereupon his father introduced him with the following words, "This is my second son. He doesn't know very much, but he studies hard and is getting better and better everyday."

The guest smiled, bowed to them both, and remarked, "He is growing superbly; he will be a source of great pride for you some day."

All were quiet for a few moments, reflecting on what had been said and what had taken place. With what might have been a sigh, the host turned and poured more tea into his friend's cup. They both sipped in silence. Then, placing his cup with a tiny, definitive click on the lacquered surface of the table, the old sensei clapped his hands and called out for his youngest son.

As youngest sons often are, he was a little slow in responding to his father's call. At the last minute he tried to make up for his tardiness and ran the rest of the way to the door. As he slid it to one side and dashed into the room, the heavy vase toppled down, striking him a tremendous blow on the head. As it did, it bounced slightly, and during that instant the youngest son whipped around like a bolt of lightning, drew his sword and slashed the vase in half before it hit the tatami floor. He was so angry, he didn't feel any pain. The vase lay in tiny bits all over the room, shattered by the blow. The boy sheathed his short sword without bothering to clean it properly and gave all those present a happy, but sheepishly embarrassed, grin. "This is my youngest son," said the old sensei with a broad, affectionate smile. "As you can see, he still has a lot to learn."

"Ah so," replied his old friend. "Still, he is very fast and very strong."

During the remainder of the afternoon, their father's honored guest spoke to all three sons, asking them about their school and teachers. He joked and talked seriously in turn, and so fascinated were the three sons by their father's old comrade-in-arms that, before they knew it, daylight was fading and their guest rose to take his leave.

It was his custom to give small gifts to his friends before going home, and he beckoned to the three sons. To the eldest he bowed very low and presented to him a marvelous gold pin with a small diamond in the center. He then looked him long in the eyes but said not a word.

To the second son he bowed very low and presented to him a heavy book, bound in magnificently tooled leather, saying, "The pages of this book are blank, as the pages of your life are blank. What you write in it is up to you."

To the third son also he bowed very low, and presented to him a beautifully polished silver pocket watch saying, "If you wish to learn, you must start by being aware of time. Then you cannot use it wrongly, even if you do nothing."

The two old senseis then embraced each other in the martial arts manner, and the honored guest departed, leaving both sorrow and joy behind him.

The black circle

In the old days, the martial arts were highly secretive, and practitioners would go to great lengths to guard their private techniques. Such techniques are the hardest to attain, for they require far more skill and practice than most students have the stamina to work for.

There is a story exemplifying this devotion to improvement. It concerns a very famous Japanese sword master named Bokuden who was a prime example of a lifetime of practice. No one could match him in a sword fight. When he became an old man, he devoted his time to teaching the art of the sword; some of the most venerated names in samurai history were students of the teacher Bokuden.

A Zen-trained sword fighter, he accepted his students in the typical Zen manner, testing their patience by making them wait for two years before they could begin training. One of his students spent a period of six months, after his final acceptance, doing nothing but cleaning and working for the master in his kitchen. After a half year of this, the student's patience was at an end, and he asked the master when he would be instructed in sword handling. The student vehemently exclaimed that his only desire in life was to be a swordsman and that he did not think that the great Bokuden was teaching him to become one. At this, the old Zen master looked into the eyes of his student and replied that they would begin lesson two the next day.

That night, as the student lay asleep, the sword master attacked him with a bamboo stick, thrashing him viciously. Subsequently, the student would be working, and suddenly in the heat of a summer's day the master would attack him with all his vigor. Any time the student was not on the alert or was trying to relax, he would be attacked or hit with a stick. Eventually, the master began to use the flat of his sword in the surprise attacks. For several years, not a word passed between the master and the student, but every time the master saw him, he would attack.

When the student was finally able to carry a sword himself, he practiced blocking the master's attacks under every condition. The student eventually got to the point in his training where, although he might be sound asleep, he would instinctively jump up as the danger of the master's sword descended upon him. After much time had passed, he reached the stage where he could draw his sword in time to fend off the attacks. At this point, the master finally spoke to him.

He told the student to meet him early the next morning, for he would have something of value for him. When he met the master the next day, he was presented with a magnificent diploma, a piece of white rice paper with a black circle drawn on it. When Bokuden presented it to his graduated student, he said to him the following words, "This black circle represents the mirror of your mind. Now you are a swordsman." With this, the swordsman left the house of the great master forever. That particular diploma became very famous through the reputation of the student who earned it, for he came to be known as the fastest sword fighter of the Tokugawa period. His name was Miamoto Musashee.

The methods of Zen masters like Bokuden were based on the empirical system of learning. Their thinking was not limited to the learning of preconceptions; their students were taught by having their instincts aroused so that they attained skill instead of academic training in preconceived ideas. In the Bushido (the way of the Bushi, or warrior), it was taught that "one can achieve Nirvana through one's own iron will." Students were taught never to surrender to circumstances. That is why they were capable of doing the fantastic deeds common in the battles of those times.

A team of inferior sword handlers were not able to cope with one superior samurai. In feudal Japan, the samurai warrior was considered a member of the noblest and most honorable profession. The samurai way was jealously guarded and was handed down in families from generation to generation. There was an apprenticeship system much like that of the feudal knights in Europe. An aspiring and eligible youth would serve a period of learning and servitude to a samurai master, living the life of a disciple for many years while his master taught him the art of the samurai.

The red arrow

There was a dojo in Yokohama, Japan, that was never paralleled for outstanding exhibitions. The master of the dojo was highly skilled in several arts, including stick fighting and archery. In typical shows of the past, he would display his versatility to all by performing amazing feats. He would take inch-thick pine boards and throw them up in the air with his left hand, then snap them in half with a short right jab while they were still in mid-air. He would then repeat the process by breaking another six boards with his left hand. This feat is rarely seen in board-breaking exhibitions, for it requires great skill: only the very fastest jabs can snap an unsupported board in half while it is descending in mid-air.

Perhaps the sensei's most amazing quality was his perceptivity; by merely studying a person's face for a few seconds, he could determine the individual's character type. He demonstrated this skill yearly in an exhibition which became famous because of its red arrow.

As the master was performing a kata, he would skirt past a rack on the dojo wall which held a long archery bow.

While still moving in the kata forms, he would remove it from the wall and, with the same gliding step, take a red arrow and spin around toward the audience. He would then fire the arrow, which would bury itself in the cherry wood beam over the doorway, hitting just two inches above the head of an unsuspecting spectator. The fantastic thing was that, without fail, the sensei would aim above the head of an armed man; he picked a gangster or a policeman every time. The audience, who relished this type of show, eagerly awaited each annual performance, for they were anxious to know at whom the archer would aim.

He would often demonstrate his skill by applying his techniques to the sword, drawing it lightning fast. As he drew it, he would slice a Japanese radish in half. The vegetable was pressed against the bared chest of one of his students; the slice of the knife would cut the radish completely in half and not even touch the body of the student. With the same circular sweep of the sword, the master would then return the blade to the scabbard. It was all done so fast that few in the amazed audience would have time to notice that the click of the hilt tightening to its shield coincided with the dull thud of the vegetable on the floor. It required fantastic skill and speed to do this. Even though it is unlike Japanese audiences to applaud, they did so vociferously.

These shows usually lasted for over two and a half hours. Visitors would occasionally demonstrate their own martial art; superiority was determined by a person's versatility. The show always ended when the sensei, with blazing eyes and a deafening scream, would run barefooted up an inverted V-shaped sword rack. It held a total of eleven blades, all with the cutting edge highly honed and pointed upwards. As he ran down the other side, lightning fast, he would jump up in the air with a terrific yell which preceded his landing to a squat position on the floor. There was never a mark on him. Even to this day there are old senseis in Japan who are able to perform this feat.

The emperor's champion

There was a time when a famous Shinken Shobu (fight to the death) occurred between the grand champion of China and the best fighter in a small Asian kingdom. At that point in history, the Mongolian emperor was encamped on the outskirts of that small kingdom with his military forces. He was skeptical about an outright and immediate attack on the people there, for he knew that the treacherous terrain of the country would cause a great loss of men and animals. Then too, the inhabitants were particularly fierce warriors, and, although they were few in number, they would be fighting for love of their king and their land.

The emperor, who wanted to conquer this small land without having to pay heavily for it, had learned a great deal about the people and their leader through his intelligence sources. He knew that the king was a martial arts devotee like himself. He knew that the people were energetic and robust like their king. He also knew that the king was reasonable. The emperor, hoping to take the land with as little bloodshed as possible, arranged for a meeting with the reigning leader; a conference immediately ensued between the two great men.

The Mongolian asked for the outright surrender of the kingdom with no resistance. This was his first overture in their bargaining procedure as great gentlemen; it was an understandable gesture, for he knew that the king realized that the emperor's forces had the power to conquer his land. The king bargained with the emperor with the utmost calm and confidence. He seemed to be tolerating the presence of the hordes of Chinese with their horses and smelly camels. The king knew that the emperor was a martial arts devotee and that he had the Chinese grand champion in his personal company at that time. The king told the emperor that he would pay him a tribute of the wealth of the land without a battle, provided that the Chinese troops would at no time set foot into the kingdom. They could consider it a token victory without any occupation of troops. The Mongolian, who was a shrewd bargainer, was surprised at this quick offer by the king. He pondered the proposal for a moment and then, with a bit of humor, suggested that, since they were both adherents of the martial arts, perhaps the best of each side could fight a battle. He proposed that, if the best fighter in the kingdom could defeat the Chinese champion, he would give his word of honor that there would be no occupation by his troops.

The king was forced to agree to this—there was no choice. The emperor was a rather cruel person, and, immediately after the king gave his consent to the arrangement, the emperor interjected that, if the Chinese champion should win the battle, the king must also forfeit his wife and daughters to become the personal slaves of the emperor. In this way, the king would be insured that there would be neither occupation of his country nor bloodshed. The king flushed with rage at this, but, keeping complete control of his regal manners, he casually agreed. He would have the best martial arts fighter in the kingdom meet the Chinese champion at the appointed time and place for a fight to the death. The emperor was thrilled, for he enjoyed watching his champion fight more than anything in the world.

When the two fighters met, everyone, especially the emperor, was amazed; the very best fighter in the kingdom was the king himself. The king performed a famous technique of kicking which ended the battle immediately. The Chinese champion died from two flying kicks directed into the eye and temple of his head. The Mongolian emperor was so dumbfounded by the fact that the king was the champion of his own country that he, the emperor, personally bowed down to the other royal person out of respect and humility.

The Mongolian subsequently left the land with his armies, never to return. To this very day, that small kingdom has never been occupied by troops from a foreign land. The name of that kingdom was Siam.

Fingers Charlie

At one time on the waterfront district of Honolulu there was a unique character who called himself the strongest man in the world. He made his living by destroying inanimate objects for the entertainment of spectators, feats which no other person in the world could equal.

In his youth he had been a martial arts student and had become so fascinated with a particular Chinese art form that he practiced that technique, to the exclusion of all others, all his life. It was the single finger stabbing technique known as "nukite." He had developed the strength in a single finger of each hand so effectively that he was able to use it as a spear tip: he was actually able to poke holes into tin cans with one strike of his finger. The two fingers looked as if they had formed into blunted spikes. Claiming that with only his two fingers he could defeat anyone, he often challenged the other martial arts men on the island to a duel. Needless to say, he was never matched.

One would frequently see him seated on the piers of the docks practicing with a two-and-a-half pound barbell ring. Holding it in one hand, he would stab it incessantly with the tip of his finger of the other hand. This unusual individual never had an enemy in Honolulu although many were envious of his ability. As time went by and his fame spread, the people of the area became proud of their "landmark" and bestowed on him the nickname "Fingers Charlie," and he has been known by this proud title ever since.

The Chinese baby

Once upon a time in the days of old Nippon, there lived a very proud and strong fighter, the greatest in all that island country. Everyone, even the emperor, marveled at his strength.

"Surely you are the greatest fighter in the world," all would tell him. "And surely I am," he would boastfully agree. And so it went until he was quite puffed up indeed.

One day he chanced to meet a small foreigner, a China-man, who also marveled at his prowess, saying, "Surely you are the greatest fighter in this little island country." At this, the big man rose in rage and bellowed, "What do you mean? I am the greatest in the world."

The great fighter was then speechless, for he had not realized that the world extended beyond the shores of the island empire.

At last he demanded of the little stranger, "Who is greater than I? Where are there stronger fighters?"

The little man then turned to the sea and, pointing to the horizon, said, "Beyond that line is the world, and in that world is a land far, far larger than yours. In that land there is a fighting art which has the most skilled fighters in the world. They are humble people, but they are better than you!"

The Japanese champion was stunned into silence, but he realized that to attack this upstart little foreigner would solve nothing. After a few moments of reflection, he declared, "I do not believe you. I am the greatest fighter in the world without question, but I am curious to see why you think as you do, so I shall travel to this land you speak of and see for myself."

The Japanese fighter said that he would take his own small boat on the voyage; perhaps the Chinese gentleman would honor him by giving him a few directions? The Chinese gentleman would, and the champion set out on his journey.

Upon reaching the shores of Cathay, the champion thrust his way through the people, eagerly asking everyone he met, "Who is the champion fighter of the country and where can I find him?" His search soon led him to the door of a little house in the mountains.

The door was opened by a frail Chinese grandmother, who listened politely to the gruff Japanese champion and then told him softly that it was her grandson whom he was looking for. Her grandson was only a baby but was indeed considered the best fighter in China. Would the Japanese gentleman care to wait? The baby would be coming home soon, and then they could fight together. The grandmother excused herself and went to prepare tea for the visitor and rice for the baby, explaining that the baby was always hungry when he came home from a hard day's training in the mountains. Well satisfied, the guest sat down calmly and listened to the sounds of the grandmother's preparations in the kitchen. He felt sure that he could defeat this ridiculous Chinese baby and gain recognition as the greatest fighter in the world. In a little while the champion chanced to glance out the window. As he did, he saw a great shadow slowly coming around the mountain, darkening everything in its path.

The trembling of the ground and the thumping of giant footsteps sent the visitor running into the kitchen in bewilderment. His eyes beheld the old woman setting out a cup and saucer that were as big as a bathtub. "What is that?" he demanded. "Oh, this is the cup for the baby's tea. He is coming now," replied the grandmother quietly.

The Japanese gentleman did not answer, but hastily dashed outside. His alarm changed to terror when he caught sight of the Chinese baby, who stood towering over the trees looking down at him. The Japanese champion turned and rushed down the mountain side as fast as he could.

"Wait," cried the grandmother, "there will be plenty of time to fight after you both have tea!"

The visitor did not answer. His one thought was to get to his boat, which was anchored on the beach at the bottom of the mountain, and start for home. At last he reached it, jumped in, and began rowing madly for Japan. In his haste he had forgotten to take in the anchor, which was on the beach, and he flailed the water with the oars to no avail. The baby soon appeared on the shore and, booming out, "Come back and fight," stepped into the ocean and gave a mighty tug on the anchor line. With that, the boat and the

127

Japanese champion flew through the air like an arrow, hitting the baby in the forehead and knocking him to the ground.

Stunned, the baby picked himself up and, seeing his challenger running across the field, started out in hot pursuit, crying, "Wait, wait, we'll sit and talk first! Maybe we could play together!" The very idea of playing with this baby terrified the fighter, but he had run a long way and was beginning to tire. The great baby soon overcame him and reached out to scoop him up in his powerful hands. Luck was with the Japanese visitor a second time, for just then the baby tripped on a large boulder, somersaulted through the air, and fell head first into a stone well, which was in the center of the village. There he remained stuck, his great baby feet waving in the air.

The Japanese champion could hardly believe his good fortune and heaved a sigh of relief. The people of the village all bowed down to him when they saw the baby's feet waving from the well, for they thought that the visitor had done this in defeating their champion fighter. The champion said nothing and went about returning to his own country.

When he finally arrived, after repairing his boat and rowing all the way, he was greatly honored and congratulated, as the glorious news of his victory had preceded him. He had had a great deal to think about on the way home, and everyone was amazed to see that he had become quiet and modest. He had learned that things often are not what they seem to be and that the world is a far larger and more complicated place than one island.

The Chinese boxers

As a result of the Boxer Rebellion, the high martial arts standards of the old days have been lost to history. The real patriots of China, who wanted Chinese solidarity even to the point of defying the wishes of their beloved empress, were the proud martial arts masters of the country. The nickname given to these leaders by the press of the world was "boxers": it was a case of unarmed men against armed men, of iron will power against explosives. These men, who had to contend with internal hazards and the disapproval of the reigning powers, fought with spears and "chi" against machine guns and cavalry.

In those days, the martial arts were at the peak of excellence; the various clans and systems and masters united their forces for war. The foreign soldiers of the armies fighting in China were amazed by the incredible deeds of the boxers. Despite the overwhelming odds against them, the martial arts men fought to the death; their heroism was as great as their ferocious fighting ability. Because of this dedication to the principle of fighting for their beliefs, all the great masters were killed. World and local opinion did not consider them righteous in their zeal and rationalized its action of gunning the boxers down with the assumption that they were inhuman. Although dynamite and machine guns eventually triumphed, they did so at a terrific cost, for many great men perished in the struggle.

The bartender's knife

*T*he Chinatown district of
Yokohama has long been famous for its lively entertainment strip, which caters to the pleasure of tourists and
servicemen. One hot summer night, not too many years
ago, a seamen's sayonara party was taking place in one of
the clubs; all the party girls were singing and entertaining
their beloved seagoing friends.

Suddenly the pleasantries of the party were interrupted
by a large seaman storming into the bar. He was carrying
a switch blade, opened, in his right hand. Shoving his way
into the throng, he yelled out the name of his girl friend
whom he knew was there with his best friend. The place
became deathly silent—the feeling of murder was in the
air. Panic and fear took hold on everyone there except one
person.

A famous Karateman, who had been quietly observing
the furious sailor, leaned over the bar and whispered to the
bartender to give him a sharp bread knife. The bartender
surreptitiously complied. As soon as the Karateman had
the knife, he screamed at the top of his voice, "Hey you,
with the knife!" making a sound that could nearly shatter

the eardrums. At this, the startled seaman whirled around and stared at the Karateman at the far end of the bar.

Just at that moment, the Karateman hurled the long bread knife at the seaman: it stuck in the floor directly in front of him. The seated Karateman then intoned in a calm commanding voice, "Pick up the bread knife. You are going to need it because I am going to kill you now with my hands." Whereupon the blustering, bullying sailor lost all his nerve and, dropping his own knife, he bolted for the door and was never seen again in that part of town.

The gaiety of the party was immediately restored, as a hearty laugh was enjoyed by all. But the Karateman's visit to the bar that night has never been forgotten by the few who realized the enormity of what he did. He prevented a murder with nothing more than what Karatemen call the "true kiai." His name is Richard Kim.

Tales of Professor Wong

In the Chinatown section of Yokohama, there lives an elderly gentleman named Professor Wong. In spite of his seventy-two years, he has an ageless quality and is as alert and as strong as he was in his youth. His eyes sparkle, and his powerful voice, which retains a trace of British accent, commands attention and respect. He is a graduate of St. John's University of China and is at home in both Western and Oriental cultures, speaking Chinese, Japanese, English, and Greek. Professor Wong was born in Hawaii, served in U.S. intelligence during World War II, and later worked his way around the world as a merchant mariner.

During the war, the ship Professor Wong was on was separated from its convoy during a terrible storm. Alone and defenseless, it was prey for a Japanese destroyer squadron; fortunately it was merely captured and taken intact as a prize of war. The entire crew was placed in a prisoner of war camp.

The Japanese hated their enemies, as do all peoples at war, but their hatred was especially intense toward their Chinese captives. Professor Wong did not succumb to circumstances, but disciplined himself to take an interest in the hard labor he performed each day and amused himself by watching the Japanese soldiers in martial arts training. He soon formulated a plan to improve his position in the camp.

One day a group of guards were practicing judo near Wong's work area. He began calling out degrading remarks until he had their attention, whereupon he insulted them more strongly, loudly criticizing their weaknesses; he thus produced the desired injury to their egos. The trainees could not tolerate such impertinence from a prisoner, especially a Chinese. If the colonel had not insisted that the camp be conducted in strict accordance with the Geneva Convention's regulations, the Japanese guards would have killed him. Instead, the biggest member of the group came up to cuff Wong's ears, but before anyone knew what had happened, the aggressor's arm was broken. Four more men immediately jumped Wong but could subdue him only with the help of the column guard's rifle. The story of Wong's feat and the disgraceful tactics used by the Japanese judo men in quieting Wong spread quickly among the prisoners. This incident was a great booster for their morale and courage.

From that time on, Wong attracted the attention of the Japanese, for they respected his ability. Gradually, his captors began to match him against their own men, and eventually he fought the top man in every martial art practiced by the personnel in the camp. Curiosity quickly changed to admiration and then to awe. The professor did not lose a match.

The Chinese prisoner's victories were finally brought to the attention of the colonel himself, and Wong congratulated himself on the success of his plan. The colonel was proud of his ability as a stick fighter and decided to fight his prisoner, both because he had never fought a Chinese before and because he had never lost a match. That was the challenge. A few days later the colonel sent his aide to inform Wong that he would be required to fight a duel with the head of the camp. The professor consented with a great smile and a nod of agreement. The time had come.

The match, which was held in the judo hall of the enlisted men's barracks, stimulated great excitement. Wong took his time in donning his equipment; he was ceremonious and extremely polite. The colonel sensed that this was not to be an ordinary fight. Each man bowed in respect to his opponent and assumed his starting position. Professor Wong allowed the colonel to direct a series of strikes to his head and shoulders and then, with a sparkling smile, he bowed again to the colonel and proceeded to beat him unmercifully. Everyone in attendance was stunned into a silence of awe and fascination. Here was a case of a prisoner publicly beating the commandant of a POW camp.

Few people learned how badly Wong had beaten the colonel, for many tried to protect his reputation. In the Japanese culture it is considered a loss of face for a master to be beaten by an unknown opponent. To remain a superior fighter, one must be overwhelmed by a superior opponent; the more powerful the force against one in a fight, the less face there is to lose if he is beaten, for what man can withstand the typhoon?

A lifetime friendship developed from this match. Wong was given complete freedom of the camp and the use of its officers' facilities in exchange for his services as a coach for the camp personnel. He used his influence to persuade the guards to do special favors for the other POWs of his group.

Professor Wong's favorite technique is one which allows him to sense physical moves by his opponents before they happen. When he is fighting, it appears to viewers that he is committing no positive actions against his opponents. He is capable of instantly blocking the strongest and fastest blows of a highly conditioned athlete; but Wong does not just counter. The hand he uses to block seems to stay attached to the hand of his opponent. His attackers usually punch out almost instinctively with their free hand in desperation, and the same thing happens to that hand. These shadow techniques, called "pag-wa," completely disorient an antagonizer.

Wong's moves involve such little physical strength that the average athletic fighter finds it incomprehensible, for Wong seems to stay glued to him without effort, his body following every move the aggressor makes. Many have tried to kick and grab the little Chinese professor and in so doing put themselves off-balance. This is exactly what Wong waits for. At that moment, with a piercing yell and concentrated strength, he shoves his opponent. The force is applied in the direction of the off-balance. His opponents then smash violently to the ground or wall, usually head first if the professor is angry.

While a youth in China, Professor Wong trained in a

dojo using unorthodox training methods. Spirals and concentric circles were painted on the floor. The students would trace the lines in their foot movements and training dances to learn to "go with" all kinds of movements and forces. They were able to twist and turn so fast and so skillfully that they dissolved the force directed at them before any harm could be done. Sneaking up on a pag-wa practitioner in order to shove him from behind was as effective as charging into a fog bank. Not only did the victim's motions protect him, but the very same action caused the opponent to receive the physical force he was expending. That is why small, frail-looking pag-wa practitioners are able to defeat gigantic men. They are skilled in ingenious techniques for fighting several men at one time and are able to smash two or more opponents into each other. The more opponents they have and the harder the fight, the easier it is to win.

Occasionally, Professor Wong would get calls at his home from martial arts students who had heard the stories of the professor's feats and wanted to see for themselves the little Chinaman who could beat huge men into insensibility. Many of the students were large and muscular and held a high opinion of their own toughness. It was difficult for them to believe that anyone smaller than they could be overpowering.

On one occasion, a young Tokyo "tough guy," curious about the famous professor, decided to visit him and to destroy the myth about his great power. This would add to the prestige of the so-called "hip set" in Tokyo. He and two of his friends strolled through the streets of Chinatown in the customary manner of bullies, asking directions to the professor's house. To their surprise, they were ignored or stared down by everyone they met. This unnerved them a bit, for they were accustomed to frightening people. Finally, an old man gave them directions with a terrible, lurking smile on his lips. As the boys walked off, they saw him rub his hands together with satisfaction, chuckling to himself.

When they arrived at the professor's house, they were greeted by an exceptionally beautiful girl, whose loveliness immediately unnerved them. She inquired what they wanted; their reply sent her into gales of laughter. It occurred to the bullies that she was ridiculing them and they became extremely nervous; their plan to be gruff and forceful was failing. While they were standing in the doorway, Professor Wong suddenly appeared.

The three toughs were surprised by Wong's unprepossessing appearance. But upon closer inspection, they noticed Wong's large forearms and immense hands; the second and third knuckles of each hand were five times the size of normal ones. Despite their size and distortion, his hands were smooth, clean, and well cared for.

But the boys were not impressed by Wong's muscular appearance, for they thought that they were the victims of a joke. One of the boys said, "There must be some mistake. You could not be strong enough to hurt anyone. You are too small and old." Professor Wong looked at them and listened and, after a pause, introduced himself with a smile. He received the reply, "I'm sorry to disturb you, old man. We came here to fight the big shot China-

man of these parts, not to beat up a little old guy like you."
The leader announced, "We shall leave now."

Professor Wong made no move to escort them out, but
simply stood smiling at them, which increased their dis-
comfiture. After an embarrassing silence, Wong suggested
that, since they had made such a long journey and had
suffered much anguish because of their curiosity, they
owed it to themselves to gain satisfaction. At this the leader
became angry and retorted, "OK, old goat, I shall have to
throw you down, it seems!"

The old man mirthfully said, "You shall try your best to
touch me, but I shall slam you into the stone walls of this
room." The antagonizer's face showed rage immediately.
He strutted over to the professor with his huge chest ex-
panded, walking like a muscle-bound duck. Wong just
stood where he was, hands behind his back with a serenely
contemptuous smile.

The next thing anyone knew, the leader was doing a
break-fall off the wall. This was a new experience for him,
for he only knew how to fall on mats. He had been slammed, but not too hard, for he was able to regain his standing position. Brushing himself off, he addressed Wong
loudly. "You are lucky, old goat. I see you know something of judo yourself, and you saw that I was off balance.
This time I shall have to smash you."

The leader stalked back to Professor Wong, who again
stood still, smiling evilly. His confidence infuriated his
opponent, who attacked this time with all his might and
craftiness. But Wong slammed him again, so quickly and
skillfully that the boy was driven head first into the wall

and lost consciousness. Meanwhile, the leader's two friends stood frozen and gaping by the front door, their knees knocking.

As a member of the merchant marine in India, Professor Wong had learned the marvelous chiropractic techniques of the mystics. He quickly and mercifully applied his knowledge in bringing the injured boy back to sensibility. Then he bent and whispered in the boy's ear, "Are you satisfied with your visit?" The boy sheepishly replied that he was and rose to join his friends at the door. They all stood with heads bowed and eyes cast on the floor, feeling that they would have taken a thousand beatings rather than endure such humiliation. The little professor spared them as much embarrassment as possible. Before leaving, the leader asked him if he would accept them as pupils so that they could learn his fighting system. Wong agreed and told them to return the next day and he would talk to them about becoming students.

All three were at Professor Wong's house the next afternoon with fine gifts. Again they were met by the lovely, enigmatic girl, but there was no laughter as before. She informed them that the professor was not at home, but that they could wait for him in the living room if they wished.

About mid-afternoon she served them tea. As evening approached, she said that Professor Wong still had not returned and that they should return the next day. The three boys were annoyed because they were immaculately dressed and impeccably groomed so as to please the professor.

The next day two of the boys came back; one of them

had lost interest. By noon another became impatient and said to his companion, "This Chinese professor must be crazy because nobody could be so strong in such a small body and be sane." He then said that when the old man had hit the leader, he seemed merely to be flexing his hands out of some sort of weird circular blocking move and that the piercing yell which accompanied this seemed to be that of a demon. Convinced that the old man was an insane wizard, the second boy left.

The leader was left to wait alone. Once more the girl announced that he should return the next day. He accepted this calmly and left.

Again he returned and was admitted by the lovely girl, who seemed very pleased to see him. She smiled and spoke with him all morning, confessing that she was Professor Wong's daughter. As the hours passed, they developed a beautiful relationship. It proved to be a very rare morning, such as one experiences seldom in a lifetime.

At the stroke of noon, the door to the main part of the house opened and the professor entered. The prospective student greeted the old man and Professor Wong replied, "Ah, I see you have patience." The boy smiled to himself at his victory. "That is good," continued the professor, "for now I shall take you as my student." Those words began a relationship that lasted for the rest of their lives. The student eventually married the professor's daughter, and the old man became the grandfather of eleven happy children.

Author's critique of the contemporary Karate scene

I believe that there is no intrinsically superior martial art, martial style, or even a truly superior practitioner. We are all students for life, but there is the ever-present hazard, especially true for beginners, of forgetting this truth.

The Oriental masters in particular are notorious for their inability to work together as equals. American practitioners tend to fall into this bad habit. There is the tendency for cultism to develop and replace the real meaning of martial arts training. Often great teachers lose themselves and their art by succumbing to the worship of students who have become followers, rather than seekers.

Petty jealousies and squabbles over meaningless points of interpretation and over precedence in the hierarchy of established greats feed upon themselves and eventually destroy all hopes of unification and central organization. Unorganized and without generally accepted fundamental standards, Karate has not yet been admitted to the Olympic games as an official sport.

Karatemen, by training and by nature, are notoriously

egocentric individualists. An approach to obtaining a minimum consensus must accommodate the inherently individual nature of the art. The attempts at resolving the contrary aspects of the situation have not yet been successful. No style has ever bowed to the dictates of another style. No Karate organization wants to submit to regulation that would in any way inhibit true feelings or private interpretation. Karate no longer is the exclusive property of the Oriental. This has resulted in a degree of resentment, natural but regrettable, which adds to the problem.

Organizations in Japan, Korea, Okinawa, United States, and Europe are vying for international sanction as a controlling body. All, in the final analysis, are profit motivated.

Invariably, disciples of great masters and systems eventually break away and form their own systems. This tendency, quite natural when charismatic leaders appear, will always be a hazard. Hopefully, it can be countered in some way. Martial arts training produces charismatic characters. Just as in life, children grow up, the times change, old values lose favor, new discoveries and breakthroughs in learning occur; it is a perpetual cycle.

Tight local organization has been typical of the Karate dojo. For international organization, rigid organization is neither feasible nor desirable. Individual masters must meet and arrive at a consensus. Once accomplished, such consensus would pave the way to a liberal, but systematic organization sufficient to qualify Karate as an event in international sports spectacles.

No czar, no president, no cultism, no singular figurehead could ever succeed in unifying Karatemen for any purpose. Karatemen have no fear, therefore force is useless in controlling them. Karatemen feel about their practice and style the way religious people feel about their religion. The motives and emotions are comparable, as is the problem of organization.

Karatemen should come to understand that they can unify for the limited purpose of entering internationally recognized competitive events. With such limited purpose, the central organization need be vested with only such powers as are necessary to such purpose. Federation would be an unnecessarily centralized approach, giving inherent and implied powers to the central governing body. But the concept of "confederation," by which the central body wields only those powers freely granted by the member groups, seems to be a quite reasonable approach—one which could solve the problems without throwing the baby out with the bath water.

The dan system as used in Karate is inconsistent in a way which contributes nothing to the individual and private aspects of the art. Ratings are relative; not all styles terminate in the same number. A style that terminates at five or eight is on an over-all level of excellence with one that terminates at ten. In a Karate organization encompassing all styles, the rated practitioners of each individual organization should be capable of competing on even terms with their counterparts in other organizations. If consensus were reached on a standard rating system, competition would insure that all organizations use similar standards. An organization which gave undeserved promotions would soon be laughed out of existence.

Every true master of a style feels that his and his alone is the best in the world. Human feelings won't change, but at least all can restrain their egos. It is true that we each achieve "satori" in our own way; however, the ego is a component of the psychological environment, and the decisions of the ego are enacted in the operational environment. If we can arrange to test our "satori" in the operational environment of competition on even terms with the "satori" of a rival school, our egos might be beneficially adjusted to reality. But we can always preserve our illusion, today, by simply refusing the even terms. This hardly accords with my concept of the Karateman.

The adoption of minimum standards for rating and competing would eventually cause each Karateman and each system to stand or fall on the basis of excellence. Today, it is all too easy for Karatemen to trade upon the reputation of past masters of their school and to capitalize upon a fortuitous membership in nation or race enjoying the mystique of organization of the art.

Standards for rating and competing are not essential to the individual pursuit of excellence. But they are essential to providing an environment which will permit the individual to test his degree of excellence. Should such consensus be achieved, the problems would remain of avoiding chauvinism, dictatorship through personality worship, and loss of democracy through messiah-seeking. A rational approach to system in Karate may take a long time, but we should never forget—"Nothing is Impossible."